CW00539235

The Pilgrim's Progress:
A Curriculum for Schools

Based on the book by John Bunyan (1628-1688).
Written and compiled by Ruth J Broomhall

The stained glass window contains the following text on its banners:

ON A CERTAIN PLACE WHERE THERE WAS A DEN AND LAID
LIGHTED ME DOWN
WORLD IN THAT
OF THIS PLACE TO
WILDERNESS THE SLEEP AND
THROUGH AS I SLEPT
WALKED DREAMED
AS I A DREAM

IN COMMEMORATION OF THE TERCENTENARY OF THE PUBLICATION
OF THE PILGRIMS PROGRESS ON THE 18th FEBRUARY 1678.

'As I walked through the wilderness of this world, I lighted on a certain place, where was a den. And I laid me down in that place to sleep. And as I slept I dreamed a dream. I dreamed, and behold I saw a man clothed with rags, standing in a certain place, with his face from his own house, a book in his hand and a great burden upon his back.'

4

John Bunyan's Hymn

Who would true valour see
Let him come hither;
One here will constant be,
Come wind, come weather.
There's no discouragement
Shall make him once relent,
His first avow'd intent
To be a pilgrim.

Who so beset him round
With dismal stories,
Do but themselves confound;
His strength the more is;
No lion can him fright,
He'll with a giant fight,
But he will have a right
To be a pilgrim.

Hobgoblin, nor foul fiend,
Can daunt his spirit;
He knows he at the end
Shall life inherit.
Then fancies fly away,
He'll fear not what men say;
He'll labour night and day
To be a pilgrim.

John Bunyan 1628-1688

These verses are found in
The Pilgrim's Progress: Part II.
They were not originally
written for use as a hymn
as singing in church was
not common in Bunyan's
time.

Musical versions of Bunyan's
hymn, including some
showing illustrations from
The Pilgrim's Progress, can be
found on the internet.

"I would wholeheartedly recommend *The Pilgrim's Progress* as a resource for schools. The curriculum planning which has been researched and written by Ruth brings this important story to life, and the children in my own school benefitted enormously from many of the ideas and activities contained within the document. The Year 6 children who worked with Ruth still talk most enthusiastically about the story, as well as the work they completed.

Richard Knowles,
Deputy Head teacher and Year 6 class teacher,
Livingstone Primary School, Bedford

Recommendations

"Working in Bedford, the home of John Bunyan, means it's even more important that the teaching of *The Pilgrim's Progress* is of both a high quality and is also very succinct for our pupils. Having taught *The Pilgrim's Progress* for a number of years I've always felt the story enables a great deal of creativity – we've visited the Saltmine Theatre, had guest speakers in and re-enacted parts of the story ourselves through role play and the impact on learners was very positive. Although I've always found that the children engage very well with the story some find the narrative difficult to follow in parts. Ruth's work carefully balances the facts around the story alongside the needs of the modern teacher. The cross referencing, suggested activities and enrichment opportunities means the learners not only engage with the subject matter but they have the chance to become creative with their learning as well and this cements the national as well as the local appeal of the programme of study. I look forward to working with this scheme to see the impact it will have on our learners.

Michael Redmond,
Senior Teacher and R.E. Coordinator,
Beauchamp Middle School
SACRE member for Bedford Borough

"*The Pilgrim's Progress* has for many years only been surpassed by the Bible as the world's most popular book! This story has captivated generations both in Britain and across the world and continues to touch the lives of countless people today. *The Pilgrim's Progress: A Curriculum for Schools* provides a wonderful resource which brings *The Pilgrim's Progress* to life for today's children. The contents have been well researched and thoughtfully brought together in a curriculum which is both engaging and inspiring. It has already been very well received by those who have used it and will be a valuable asset for teachers and students alike.

Rev. Chris Damp,
Minister, Bunyan Meeting, Bedford,
SACRE member for Bedford Borough

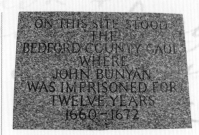

Right: Stone set into the pavement marking the site of Bedford County Gaol in Silver Street.

Did you know?

The Pilgrim's Progress was written in prison, probably during Bunyan's twelve-year term in the county gaol.

W hy study *The Pilgrim's Progress*? There are many reasons! *The Pilgrim's Progress* is a book that we should all experience. In the UK, it is part of our national and Christian heritage; world-wide it is an international bestseller with universal appeal.

It remains the third most published book in the world (after the *Bible* and *Harry Potter*). It features in the Guardian's top 100 books for 2015, passages are still read at significant national events and many famous authors have quoted it in, or used it as inspiration for, their own writing – Charlotte Bronte, C.S. Lewis, Louisa May Alcott, John Steinbeck, Mark Twain and Enid Blyton, to name just a few. In 1942 a radio version was released featuring the late Sir John Gielgud; and in 1951, an opera by Ralph Vaughan Williams. Old and new editions, versions and translations of the book, together with film and audio adaptations, continue to be enjoyed by children and adults the world over.

For Bedfordshire locally and the UK nationally Bunyan is one of the most renowned historical figureheads, not just for his most famous allegory *The Pilgrim's Progress* but for his passionate and uncompromising approach to his non-conformist beliefs and his impact on the religious and literary scenes both during his lifetime and after. Bunyan had a faith firmly grounded in the Bible, a faith that had been tried and tested from his early days as a Christian to the final days of his life. Rarely would Bunyan be allowed to enjoy a life of ease; instead he was destined to endure much pain and trouble. His eldest child was born blind and another child was stillborn, his first wife died at a young age leaving him with four children to look after and he endured two terms in prison, one of which lasted twelve years. Yet Bunyan's faith in a sovereign and providential God remained secure throughout. Driven by his own experience of God and a deeply Christian faith, his passion first and foremost was to lead others to Christ. Bunyan did this through his two main gifts – his ability to preach and his ability to write.

Bunyan's gift for writing is perhaps nowhere better demonstrated than in *The Pilgrim's Progress*. It is a story that has proved the test of time, place, culture, faith, gender, age. It is a story that is relevant to all of us because it is a story of the pilgrimage that we are all on – the pilgrimage of life. We can all identify with it, whatever race or religion, age or gender, because we are all on the journey.

But the story goes deeper than that. It is an allegory that uses a wealth of characters and symbolism, all representing persons or experiences we might encounter on our individual journeys. So, as a story, it acts as a great discussion tool for universal aspects of life – morality, behaviour, experience, belief, values etc.

But *The Pilgrim's Progress* goes even deeper than that. It is, in essence, a spiritual story, an account of one pilgrim's journey from this life to the next. The pilgrim is 'Christian' and as we read about his journey and all that he encounters, Bunyan enables us to understand what it truly means to be 'Christian'. Bunyan uses his own experience and others, together with his extensive knowledge of the Bible and mature spiritual wisdom, to create a unique and powerful account of the Christian journey from the City of Destruction (a world without God) to the Celestial City (heaven).

I have had reason to engage with *The Pilgrim's Progress* as a teacher, adviser, youth worker, godmother, aunt, foster carer and Master's student over a period of more than twenty years. As a child I was given a special copy of the book by my parents but it remained on my bookshelf, mainly unread, for over 30 years. Words written in the front of the book by my father express the hope that, next to the *Bible*, it would prove one of the most worthwhile books to read. And it has. After many years and my own rather 'dangerous journey' at times, *The Pilgrim's Progress* has proved itself especially valuable, not just to me personally but to countless children I have had the pleasure to introduce it to. It is a book and a story that I thoroughly recommend.

The Pilgrim's Progress: A Curriculum for Schools is inspired, not just by the book itself, but by the many children I have taught over the years who have responded with such interest and enthusiasm. In a society where faith, belief in God and the spiritual development of children seems to have a rapidly decreasing status, *The Pilgrim's Progress* encourages children to explore faith from both a subjective and an objective viewpoint; it enables faith to be encountered and experienced as well as learnt. And whilst it is unashamedly Christian in its teaching, it is also very inclusive, inspiring discussion on aspects of faith generally as well as specifically. It is my hope that *The Pilgrim's Progress: A Curriculum for Schools* will both encourage wider engagement with Bunyan's world-famous allegory and prove to be an invaluable resource for all schools who believe in a truly holistic approach to education.

But the last word should surely go to the audience for whom this *Curriculum* is intended – the children. Throughout this *Curriculum* I have included quotes from the children in Year 6 at Livingstone Primary School, Bedford, who studied *The Pilgrim's Progress* in the autumn term 2015. Livingstone Primary School is a multi-cultural, multi-faith school in the heart of Bedford. After some initial research into the life and times of John Bunyan, the children, teachers and I journeyed together through *The Pilgrim's Progress* from the City of Destruction to the Celestial City, using a variety of mediums (reading, listening, film, theatre and drama). The scheme of study culminated in a visit to Bunyan Meeting and the John Bunyan Museum, where the children enjoyed tours of the church and museum, enacted scenes from the story using the stained glass windows as a stimulus and interviewed biographer Peter Morden as well as John Bunyan himself (a church member in disguise!). The quotes you read throughout this *Curriculum* are the children's honest responses to their experiences.

Finally, I would like to acknowledge the support of Livingstone Primary School in allowing me to teach *The Pilgrim's Progress* during the autumn term 2015. In particular, I would like to thank Richard Knowles, deputy head-teacher and Year 6 class teacher, for his enthusiastic approach to the idea and weekly welcome; and to the children themselves, who were a fantastic class and received the story with such great interest and enthusiasm. The experience enabled me to write this *Curriculum* with a renewed belief in *The Pilgrim's Progress* and its ability to educate, inspire, motivate and impact both children and adults alike. Thank you Livingstone!

Ruth Broomhall
August 2016

Notes

The Pilgrim's Progress: A Curriculum for Schools

The title *The Pilgrim's Progress* generally refers to the story of the pilgrim Christian, written by Bunyan when in gaol and first published in 1678. The second part of his allegory – the journey to the Celestial City of Christian's wife Christiana, their four children and Mercy, a friend – is titled *The Pilgrim's Progress: the second part* or *The Pilgrim's Progress: Part II*. Editions of *The Pilgrim's Progress* do not always include the second part/Part II.

Following this general rule, for the purposes of this *Curriculum* when the title *The Pilgrim's Progress* is used it refers only to the story of Christian. Christiana's story is referred to as *The Pilgrim's Progress: Part II*.

For schools that do not follow the general UK terminology, Key Stage 1 refers to pupils aged 5-7 years (School Years 1 and 2), Lower Key Stage 2 refers to pupils aged 7-9 Years (School Years 3 and 4) and Upper Key Stage 2 refers to pupils aged 9-11 years (School Years 5 and 6).

The *Curriculum* is divided into 4 sections:

1. **Background** (to Bunyan and to the Curriculum)

2. **The Story Explained**

3. **Curriculum**

4. **Resources Information**

For ease of reference, each section is colour-coded and further divided into sub-sections. Sub-sections are listed on the title page for each section. Individual right-hand pages are labelled with the appropriate section/sub-section.

The stained glass window images used throughout the *Curriculum* are images of the windows in Bunyan's church, Bedford (Bunyan Meeting, Mill Street, Bedford). Each window tells part of Bunyan's famous allegory. Additional images are of places or artefacts relevant to the life, times and works of John Bunyan and have been kindly supplied by the John Bunyan Museum. Many of these can be seen in the Church/Museum or vicinity.

Contents

Did you know?

The Pilgrim's Progress remains in the top three most published books in the world, after the Bible and, more recently, *Harry Potter*.

Statue of John Bunyan, Bedford.

66 I really enjoyed the story which is strange because I usually don't like stories about religion and I like John Bunyan's idea to give the characters names that describe them. I enjoyed everything we did and read in these weeks. The museum was really fun and interesting because we had an opportunity to see how the prison was like and how John Bunyan lived.

Chapter 1
Background

Then said Evangelist, pointing with his finger over a very wide field, 'Do you see yonder Wicket-gate?'

The man said, 'No'.

Then said the other, 'Do you see yonder shining light?'

He said, 'I think I do.'

Then said Evangelist, 'Keep that light in your eye, and go up directly thereto, so shall you see the gate; at which when you knock, it shall be told to you what you shall do.'

1617
1618
1619
1620
1621
1622
1623
1624

◀ Charles I accedes to the throne of England. **1625**

1626
1627

1628 ◀ Birth of John Bunyan at Elstow, Bedfordshire.

1629

Above: Elstow church.

Left: Cottages in Elstow.

1630
1631
1632
1633
1634
1635
1636
1637
1638
1639
1640
1641

◀ Outbreak of English Civil War. **1642**

1643

1644 ◀ Death of John Bunyan's mother Margaret. His father remarries and John joins the Parliamentary army.

1645
1646

◀ Second Civil War. **1647** ◀ Bunyan returns to Elstow.

1648 ◀ Bunyan marries for the first time. Name of his wife is unknown but thought to be Mary.

◀ Civil War ends with execution of Charles I. A commonwealth is proclaimed. **1649** ◀ Bunyan's spiritual conversion.

1650 ◀ Birth of Bunyan's first child. Her name is Mary and she is blind.

1651

1652 ◀ Bunyan's spiritual conversion.

◀ Oliver Cromwell becomes Lord Protector. **1653** ◀ Bunyan joins the independent church meeting at St. John's Church, Bedford.

1654

◀ England divided into eleven military units. **1655** ◀ Bunyan family resident in St. Cuthbert's Street, Bedford.

1656 ◀ Publication of Bunyan's first book, *Some Gospel Truths Opened*.

1657

◀ Oliver Cromwell dies. **1658** ◀ Bunyan's first wife dies.

1659 ◀ Bunyan marries his second wife, Elizabeth.

1660
1661

John Bunyan (1628 – 1688)

A brief biography of his life, including his own spiritual journey

John Bunyan was born in the village of Elstow, Bedfordshire, in November 1628. His baptism as an infant is recorded as taking place on 30th November 1628. His actual birth date is not known for sure but is believed to have been 28th November, as christenings usually took place a couple of days after a child was born.

Bunyan's parents were Thomas and Margaret Bunyan. They were not the poorest people but times were still very hard for them. The Bunyan family lived in what was probably a fairly ram-shackle thatched cottage with a small workshop attached. John's father, Thomas Bunyan, was a tinker, a trade which John was to take up as an apprentice on his return from the English Civil War. It is thought that Thomas was illiterate (his will was signed with a simple 'x' rather than a signature) and he almost certainly was a heavy drinker and swearer, an example his son John would have been strongly influenced by as a teenager. Thomas and Margaret would have attended their local parish church regularly, as would the young John Bunyan, but this was probably more out of tradition and expectation (you got fined if you didn't) than an active belief.

In the summer of 1644 John's mother Margaret and his eldest sister (also called Margaret – it was the tradition to name the firstborn daughter after the mother) both died. Average life expectancy in Bunyan's day was only around forty years of age so such a loss, though tragic, was not uncommon. But John was still hit hard by the loss of both his mother and his sister and when his father remarried just months after, John left home and joined the Parliamentary army. The English Civil War had commenced in 1642 and boys over the age of sixteen were able to enlist. Evidence suggests John may

have been a few months short of his sixteenth birthday when he became a soldier, possibly lying about his age in order to escape an unhappy home life. (It is interesting to note that when John himself lost his first wife, he too remarried very soon after.)

Bedfordshire at that time favoured the Parliamentary cause, which is probably why Bunyan became a foot soldier in the Parliamentary army. He was mainly based at Newport Pagnell, about thirteen miles from Bedford. In 1647, two years before the end of the war, Bunyan returned to his village and his trade as a tinker. He married his first wife in 1649. We do not know the name of his first wife for certain but it is thought it was Mary as that was the name given to their first daughter. Mary Bunyan, blind from birth, was born in 1650.

> What is highly significant to the life story of John Bunyan is that his first wife came from a godly home.

They had no money but his wife did bring with her as her dowry two Puritan books which had belonged to her father. These two books were to be a great influence on John Bunyan (the fact that John could read suggests that he had attended school as a child – not a given in those days) and marked the start of a spiritual journey which led him towards a closer relationship with God and a much deeper Christian faith.

John's spiritual journey was a long and difficult one (later recorded in his spiritual autobiography *Grace Abounding to the Chief of Sinners*, published in 1666) but one which is hugely significant to his life story, his writings and his international renown and therefore important to learn in order to understand both the man and his book/s.

Above: Pencil drawing
of John Bunyan

Inspired by the books his wife had brought to their marriage, he started attending his local parish church at Elstow during the week as well as on Sundays. Unfortunately his laddish behaviour did not significantly change for the better despite this increased attendance at church. The Rev. Christopher Hall, the vicar at Elstow, preached much on sin and the consequences of bad behaviour in the sight of God. One particular Sunday he preached a sermon that was to have a huge impact on the young lad. This sermon was on the sinfulness of playing sport on a Sunday – the 'Sabbath day' – and although even this did not immediately change John's behaviour or practice, the meaning and the message clearly did not leave him. It began, for Bunyan, a growing awareness of the meaning of human sin in contrast to the perfect holiness of God (Bunyan describes this awareness in *The Pilgrim's Progress* as 'God with reference to us'). Over time, this became a personal conviction, a sense of his own inner imperfection as well as outward sinfulness (what he was as well as what he did) that was to lead to an intense spiritual struggle lasting a number of years. It compelled him to try to reform his ways and please God by being good, but the more he tried the more he struggled. Bunyan would never attain the salvation he was seeking simply by changing his behaviour for the Bible teaches that 'being good' can never be enough because of sin (what we are as well as what we do). This is the reason God sent His Son, Jesus Christ, to live on earth as man and then to die on the cross as atonement for sin. This, the Bible teaches, is the gospel – the 'good news' – of the Christian faith. But Bunyan had not yet grasped the full extent of the gospel message, and so his struggles continued.

Another significant event in Bunyan's spiritual journey came one day in Bedford, when he met 'three or four poor women sitting at a door in the sun, talking about the things of God', a scene he describes in *Grace Abounding*. He describes how he heard them talk about 'a new birth, the work of God in their hearts' and observed that 'they spoke as if joy made them speak', an experience as yet unknown to Bunyan.

> This was another crucial point in Bunyan's spiritual journey. The women were members of a church led by their founding pastor John Gifford and meeting in St. John's Church, Bedford.

Bunyan started attending the meetings at the church in Bedford and soon came to value highly the ministry and guidance of John Gifford, whom he called 'holy Mr Gifford'. It was during this time that Bunyan came to know and understand Christ as his 'Saviour' and was freed from the struggles of the past few years. Whilst he knew that the Christian life would not be one of complete ease and comfort after this, the intense spiritual struggles he had experienced in his journey to the cross had finally come to an end. The 'burden' of sin that Bunyan had felt so heavily was gone and he was free to continue his Christian life with the certainty that he was 'saved'.

The reality of his own salvation – the revelation of Christ to his soul, the forgiveness of sin, the freedom he experienced through this and the promise of an eternity in heaven – was a major turning point in Bunyan's life. It made him passionate to share his Christian faith and his spiritual knowledge and experience with others. He was soon to discover both a gift for preaching and a gift for writing, inspired and motivated by his passion for what he called 'awakening and converting work' – he wanted to see others 'saved'. This passion informed every detail of his life from then on. It was the reason he preached, the reason he would not conform to the state religion, the reason he went to prison, the reason he wrote. Bunyan believed that his faith in God must come first – before the king, before his family, before his own personal comfort – if circumstances so dictated.

They did. During the reign of Charles 1st the situation in England became very tense, with sharp differences between the King and Parliament. The strongest voice in Parliament at that time was the Puritans, who wanted more control over the King. The King, believing he was there by God's sovereign will, rallied against them. Strict laws were put in place.

Above: Bunyan preaching in Bedford, 18th October 1659.

> Preaching was not permitted except as authorised by the state church. This meant that Bunyan and other 'non-conformists' were unable to preach legally.

But Bunyan, together with many others, refused to conform to the teachings of the state church, believing that it left people in spiritual ignorance of the true gospel message. Their duty toward God as citizens of heaven came before duty to the King.

Did you know?

By the time of Bunyan's death in 1688, eleven editions of *The Pilgrim's Progress* had been published.

National Events

Restoration of the monarchy. Charles II becomes King of England. — 1660

1661

Acts of Uniformity mean that dissenting ministers (those that refuse to conform) are ejected from their livings. — 1662

1663

1664

1665

Only religious assemblies of the Church of England are allowed to meet. The Conventicle Act forbids all others. — 1666

1667

1668

Great Plague at its peak. — 1669

Great Fire of London. — 1670

1671

Charles II issues his 'Declaration of Indulgence'. — 1672

1673

1674

1675

1676

1677

1678

1679

1680

1681

Above: John Strudwick's house where Bunyan died.

1682

1683

Charles II dies. His brother, James II, becomes King. — 1684

1685

A new 'Declaration of Indulgence' is issued. The persecution of dissenters begins to ease. — 1686

1687

1688

Glorious Revolution takes place soon after Bunyan's death. — 1689

1690

William and Mary become King and Queen. The Toleration Act is passed granting significant freedom to dissenters. — 1691

1692

The life of John Bunyan

1660 — **Bunyan is arrested near Harlington, Beds, for preaching. Begins his twelve-year imprisonment in the County Gaol. The Bedford church meet in secret.**

1666 — **Publication of Bunyan's *Grace Abounding to the Chief of Sinners*, his spiritual autobiography.**

1672 — **Bunyan is released from gaol and becomes pastor of Bunyan Meeting.**

1676 — **Bunyan is imprisoned again, this time for a short period of about 6 months.**

1678 — **Publication of *The Pilgrim's Progress*.**

1682 — **Publication of *The Holy War*.**

1684 — **Publication of *The Pilgrim's Progress: Part II*.**

1688 — **John Bunyan dies and is buried in Bunhill Fields, London.**

1692 — **Elizabeth Bunyan dies.**

So Bunyan continued with his preaching engagements throughout Bedfordshire and beyond. He knew he must continue preaching the gospel message even if this meant putting his own life – and therefore that of his family – at risk. Bunyan believed firmly that God was in control of every detail of his life and if he should be arrested for preaching then God was in control of that too. This belief in God's sovereignty, during good times and bad, kept him strong both in continuing his work and in bearing the consequences of it. So, when one day in 1660 he was arrested whilst preaching and sentenced to twelve years imprisonment in the county gaol, he took his punishment graciously, refusing to give in. Indeed, he even used his time in prison to honour God – reading his Bible, preaching and witnessing to others, and writing. It is believed that it was during his twelve years in the county gaol that Bunyan was inspired to write the book that was to become his most famous work, *The Pilgrim's Progress*.

Bunyan married twice. When his first wife died, he married again soon after to Elizabeth, a family friend. Elizabeth Bunyan proved a strong and supportive wife during some very difficult times. She became mother to his four children by his first wife and bore Bunyan three more, one of which was stillborn. She stuck by him during his long years in prison and even acted as advocate for him, a sign of the strong love she had for her family, her own commitment to the Christian faith and her strength as a person. They lived in a simple cottage on St. Cuthbert's Street, Bedford and evidence suggests they enjoyed a happy marriage and a strong bond as a family, during both good times and difficult.

When Bunyan was released from prison in 1672 he was called to be the pastor of what had been Gifford's church in Bedford. A small plot of land with an orchard and a barn in Mill Street, Bedford, was purchased in the same year and licensed for preaching. Bunyan was to continue as pastor of the Bunyan Meeting church until his death in 1688. During this time he survived a second short term in prison, continued to write and travelled frequently, sometimes as far as London, on various preaching engagements. It was whilst away on one of these trips that Bunyan caught a fever and died. He was buried in Bunhill Fields, London, a burial ground of many famous Christian men and women.

> **Bunyan wrote close to 60 books in his lifetime. Whilst Bunyan's life is a thought-provoking and inspiring testament to his strong Christian faith, these books are Bunyan's real and enduring legacy.**

His most famous work, *The Pilgrim's Progress* went through 11 editions in Bunyan's lifetime and sold more than 100, 000 copies. Publishing such material at that time would have involved some level of risk (the subject matter would not always have been in agreement with the state church) and it was the publishers who mainly took on that risk and any financial benefits. Consequently Bunyan did not benefit financially but money was not his motivation. Bunyan preached in the hope that people would hear the gospel message and become 'Christian'; he wrote for the same reason. Bunyan's hope was that by writing he would reach a much wider audience. He did. His works continue to be published today, not just in Britain but world-wide, and his most famous work, *The Pilgrim's Progress*, has never been out of print. Bunyan's legacy was to be a great one, not just in his own life time but for centuries to come.

Bunyan's Literary Legacy

Bunyan's writing career started in 1656 with the publication of a book entitled *Some Gospel Truths Opened*. Ten years later, with a number of other books completed (all about the Christian faith), he published his spiritual autobiography *Grace Abounding to the Chief of Sinners*, probably his second most famous work. His most famous work, *The Pilgrim's Progress* was published in 1678 and *The Pilgrim's Progress: Part II* in 1684. His other more famous works are *Holy War* (published 1682) and *The Life and Death of Mr Badman* (published 1680). Folio editions of all his works have also been published, the first one in 1692 (this included 12 of his unpublished works).

The Pilgrim's Progress

Bunyan's most famous work is divided into two parts, although it is the first part which is by far the most famous. It is an allegory in which all the characters, places and objects are symbolic in some way to the Christian life. The story has a narrator – a dreamer – commonly thought to be Bunyan, who introduces us to the character Christian from the City of Destruction. *The Pilgrim's Progress* is the story of Christian's 'desperate journey' from the City of Destruction (symbolic of the world without God) to the Celestial City (heaven). Christian has discovered a copy of the Bible in his attic and reading it has awakened a spiritual need and curiosity which motivates him to commence his 'Christian' journey. Along the way he meets many different characters, both good and bad, and has many experiences and encounters, all of which help him to make progress towards the 'desired country' (heaven). In *The Pilgrim's Progress: Part II*, Bunyan introduces us to Christian's wife, Christiana, her four boys and her friend Mercy, and describes their journey from the City of Destruction to the Celestial City. It is a journey that Christian prayed they would take, having been distraught at having to leave them when they failed to understand or share his 'awakening' to the Bible message.

It is widely considered that Bunyan modelled his central character, Christian, on himself – hence the reason why the windows in Bunyan Meeting depicting scenes from the story show Bunyan in the role of Christian. There is much truth in this, although Bunyan would also have incorporated the experiences of many others into his allegory. Bunyan's life story (including his encounters and friendships with others) taught him much about the Christian faith and much of his symbolism is reflective of this. For example: 'Worldly Wiseman' is symbolic of Bunyan's own struggles with a traditional state religion that taught more of the importance of good works as a means

for getting to heaven than it did of the forgiveness of sins through Christ's death on the cross. 'Talkative' is symbolic of those Bunyan met who practiced an intellectual assent to Christianity but who did not understand the need to love God or the desire to follow him and aspire to a holy life. The people that Bunyan stood up against when arguing for the need for conviction of sin and an awareness of the human need for a Saviour are symbolised in the character 'Ignorance'. 'Faithful' and 'Hopeful' are symbolic of the many Christian friends and companions Bunyan himself enjoyed throughout his Christian journey, whilst 'Evangelist' represents his first pastor from the church in Bedford, the 'holy Mr Gifford'.

The Pilgrim's Progress is a story that is relevant to all ages and cultures, to all religions or none, simply because we are all on a journey through life. But it is more than that. It is a story that helps us consider our own lives from both a moral and a spiritual perspective, and to think about how faith and behaviour impacts on our own lives and those around us. More particularly (and as Bunyan would have wanted) it helps us understand the gospel message and the meaning of being 'Christian', challenging us to consider this meaning personally as well as impersonally, subjectively as well as objectively. As we read *The Pilgrim's Progress* we too can experience what it means to be 'Christian'.

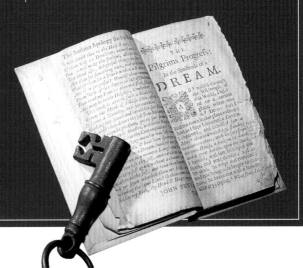

Did you know?...

Facts about *The Pilgrim's Progress*

The man and his book

The Pilgrim's Progress was written in prison, probably during Bunyan's twelve-year term in the county gaol.

Bunyan was not sure whether to publish it. He thought it might be controversial because of his use of allegory and metaphor, so he asked friends – see 'The Author's Apology' at the start of *The Pilgrim's Progress*. Although some said 'no', Bunyan decided to publish anyway.

Bunyan used Nathaniel Ponder, a publisher who was willing to take the risk. Ponder was the publisher for the Puritan John Owen. Owen was an acquaintance and keen supporter of Bunyan as well as a respected theologian with status and authority.

The Pilgrim's Progress was first published in 1678.

There were three editions of *The Pilgrim's Progress* in the space of one year (1678-9).

Bunyan made significant additions to the second and third editions only.

The third edition was the first to use illustrations.

By the time of Bunyan's death in 1688, eleven editions had been published.

Around 100,000 copies of *The Pilgrim's Progress* were published in Bunyan's lifetime.

Since its first publication in 1678 it has never been out of print.

It has been translated into more than 200 languages to date.

The Pilgrim's Progress remains in the top three most published books in the world, after the *Bible* and, more recently, *Harry Potter*.

A copy of the first edition of *The Pilgrim's Progress* is in the Bodleian Library, Oxford. A complete set of editions is in the New York Public Library.

The title *The Pilgrim's Progress* generally refers to the story of Christian's journey to the Celestial City, first published in 1678. *The Pilgrim's Progress: Part II* was published in 1684, with a second edition in 1686. It is less well-known and not always included in publications of Bunyan's *The Pilgrim's Progress*.

The Pilgrim's Progress introduces the reader to over 100 different characters, all symbolic of people we might meet on our (particularly spiritual) journey through life.

The Pilgrim's Progress: Part II tells the story of Christian's wife, Christiana, her four boys and her friend, Mercy, as they follow Christian from the City of Destruction to the Celestial City.

Bunyan's world-famous hymn, *Who Would True Valour See*, is taken from verses Bunyan wrote for *The Pilgrim's Progress: Part II*. Singing in church was not common during Bunyan's time so it is unlikely these verses were originally written for use as a hymn.

Extracts from *The Pilgrim's Progress* and *The Pilgrim's Progress: Part II* have been used in funeral services of some famous people, including Queen Elizabeth The Queen Mother, Margaret Thatcher, the UK's first woman Prime Minister and Winston Churchill, British Prime Minister during World War II.

The Pilgrim's Progress has been described as 'the Bible in another shape' (C.H. Spurgeon).

The Pilgrim's Progress makes reference to 51 out of the 66 books of the Bible. The books Bunyan refers to most are: Isaiah, Psalms, Matthew, Hebrews and Revelation; with Proverbs, Luke, John, Romans and 1 Corinthians close behind.

Bunyan would not have wanted to be famous for himself, but simply for the Christian message that meant so much to him and which he describes so vividly in the pages of *The Pilgrim's Progress*.

Using *The Pilgrim's Progress* in Schools

The Pilgrim's Progress is incredibly versatile, offering potential as a teaching resource in a variety of curriculum areas.

Did you know?

The third edition was the first to use illustrations.

The Pilgrim's Progress: A Curriculum for Schools provides comprehensive information on Bunyan's allegory and related Christian concepts, detailing some specific as well as general ideas for use, without being too prescriptive. This enables teachers/schools to adapt the *Curriculum* and the way they use the story to fit their own programmes of study as well as allowing for individual creativity in planning.

Whilst this *Curriculum for Schools* is focused on Religious Education, with a suggested ten-week 'Religious Education: Scheme of Work' for Key Stage 1, Lower Key Stage 2 and Upper Key Stage 2, the following suggestions are designed to stimulate further ideas for its use within classes, year groups, subject areas and whole school. In the majority of cases, all that teachers need to effectively teach *The Pilgrim's Progress* is an appropriate children's edition of *The Pilgrim's Progress* and a copy of *The Pilgrim's Progress: A Curriculum for Schools*. Schools may, however, choose to purchase additional resources to further enrich the learning experience (see Chapter 4: Resources Information) and/or class sets of the book to enable children to join in the reading.

For all of the ideas described here, the ten 'Story Explained' sections (see Chapter 2) are designed to enhance understanding of Bunyan's story and to help teachers bring it to life. These sections are explained in more detail in 'Using the Curriculum' (see Chapter 1.4).

ASSEMBLY/ WHOLE SCHOOL WORSHIP

The Pilgrim's Progress can be used either on its own or alongside the suggested 'Religious Education: Scheme of Work' as a resource for whole school, year group or class assembly/whole school worship time. Chapters/themes on a weekly basis can form the focus for a whole term of assemblies. The same children's edition for the whole school can be used (*The Family Pilgrim's Progress* works well) or different versions according to age/ability but keeping to the same theme. Weekly readings of chapters/themes can be replaced or enriched by using film/media versions. A weekly verse taken from the list of related verses for that particular chapter/theme could be chosen each week to further the worship/learning experience across the school.

LITERACY

The Pilgrim's Progress is an excellent book for using within the Literacy curriculum and can be the medium for studying: allegory, the historical novel, language (including comparison with 17th century language), use of poetry, script-writing, media studies (audio, film, animation, theatre versions all available). It covers skills such as speaking and listening, drama, comprehension, writing.

To enable teachers and pupils to study *The Pilgrim's Progress* in depth classes could study it as part of the RE and Literacy curriculum combined, thereby doubling the amount of curriculum time devoted to it. The book could be read as part of Literacy, leaving RE time to explore the story and related concepts; or the reading could be shared between the two leaving a more equitable distribution of time for following up skills and concepts in both subject areas.

HE HATH GIVEN ME REST BY HIS SORROW AND LIFE BY HIS DEATH

This far did I come laden with my sin,
Nor could ought ease the grief that I was in,
Till I came hither: What a place is this!
Must here be the beginning of my bliss?
Must here the burden fall from off my back?
Must here the springs that bound it to me, crack?
Blest Cross! Blest Sepulchre! Blest rather be
The Man that there was put to shame for me.

> I really enjoyed studying *The Pilgrim's Progress* and was really sad when I was sick and missed a lesson. I enjoyed studying about *The Pilgrim's Progress* and John Bunyan because it was very interesting. At first I was like 'oh no this is going to be boring' but Ruth made the learning really fun. I also really liked the idea of us going to the John Bunyan Museum. My favourite part was doing the acting at the museum. It was really funny when everyone ran to Peter Morden for his autograph.

RELIGIOUS EDUCATION

The Pilgrim's Progress is an ideal medium for teaching and learning about the Christian faith and therefore fits well within, or as an extension of/complement to, a Religious Education curriculum. Acting as a 'case study' for the Christian faith through the story of the pilgrim 'Christian', it will allow pupils to gain a comprehensive understanding of the Christian faith as part of the curriculum in its own right, or it can be used to extend and enrich existing curriculum provision. The experiential nature of the story enhances the learning experience, enabling pupils to achieve a greater depth of understanding of the Christian faith and its meaning, significance and impact on individuals and the wider world. *The Pilgrim's Progress* is therefore an ideal resource for understanding Christianity, including the text (both the story itself and the Bible), its impact on individuals, and how it relates to the wider community/world.

The suggested ten week 'Religious Education: Scheme of Work' outlined in this *Curriculum* is designed for children throughout Years 1-6, allowing for natural progression and more detailed and in-depth understanding of concepts as children mature (see the following 'Using the Curriculum' for a detailed explanation of the scheme of work). Whilst schools may choose one particular year group to use this with, there is also the potential for introducing the story in Key Stage 1 and then revisiting it in Key Stage 2 to embed and enrich the previous learning experience. Children and adults alike often enjoy reading books/stories more than once and can appreciate them in new and different ways each time. The wide range of Christian concepts covered in *The Pilgrim's Progress*, combined with Bunyan's clever symbolism and extensive use of biblical texts, means that this story is an ideal one for studying more than once.

If used alongside the RE curriculum, *The Pilgrim's Progress* can complement/support/fulfil existing themes, topics and approaches. The examples below are taken from the RE Agreed Syllabus for Bedford Borough, Central Bedfordshire and Luton 2012-2017 and are used with permission:

In **Key Stage 1**, it can be used to support study units/fields of enquiry such as:

- Who is a Christian and what do they believe?
- What can we learn from sacred books and stories?
- How do we show we care for others?
- Who is an inspiring person?

In **Lower Key Stage 2**, it can be used to support study units/fields of enquiry such as:

- How and why do believers show their commitments during the journey of life?
- How should we live and who can inspire us?
- How and why does a Christian follow Jesus?

In **Upper Key Stage 2**, it can be used to support study units/fields of enquiry such as:

- Why do some people inspire others?
- What matters most to Christians? (can be contrasted with other religions)
- Why is pilgrimage important to some religious believers?
- How do people live through good times and through hard times?

Left:
The church's 'baptising place' was in the River Ouse.

Did you know?

The Pilgrim's Progress makes reference to 51 out of the 66 books of the Bible. The books Bunyan refers to most are: **Isaiah**, **Psalms**, **Matthew**, **Hebrews** and **Revelation**; with **Proverbs**, **Luke**, **John**, **Romans** and **1 Corinthians** close behind.

More generally, during a study of *The Pilgrim's Progress* pupils will have the opportunity to develop their understanding of the Christian faith. As pupils develop their understanding of Christian faith and practice, comparisons can then be made with other faiths or belief systems. For example:

• Regarding Christian **FAITH**, they can: learn how to use a range of religious words and understand key Christian concepts; recognise what it means to be a Christian, the key aspects of Christianity and how Christian practices and ways of life stem from Christian beliefs and teachings; learn about Christian symbols and symbolism; understand Christian responses to ultimate and ethical questions.

• Regarding Christian **PRACTICE**, they can: reflect on spiritual and moral values, ideas of right and wrong, and how these relate to their own behaviour and others; consider a range of religious and spiritual feelings including love, joy, peace, sadness, grief, despair, praise; recognise that to be a Christian involves commitment and consider the challenges that come with this; reflect on what it means to be part of a faith community/ church; reflect on sources of inspiration in their own lives and others; identify what matters to them and others, including Christian/religious commitments.

A study of *The Pilgrim's Progress* can also cover a range of methodology relating to RE:

• **The phenomena of religion**: studying Christianity through Bunyan's story, considering the behaviour of 'Christian' and other pilgrims and relating these to modern life and experiences; appreciating some of the artistic expressions of the story (stained glass windows, illustrations, etc).

• **Experiential RE**: engaging with pupils own spiritual capacities through the text, encouraging personal and shared reflection of thoughts, experiences and interpretations.

• **Interpretive RE**: relating the story and the 'Christian' experience of pilgrimage as narrated by Bunyan with what is known of Christianity today. Consider similarities and differences and the reasons for them, together with similarities and differences between Christian groups/denominations today.

• **Concepts for Learning**: key Christian concepts covered through the story include God as Trinity, sin and salvation, the gospel message, Christ's death on the cross and the resurrection, conversion, heaven and hell, the Bible as the Word of God, angels, the devil/good and evil, the church/Christian community and prayer; also the Christian response to doubt and suffering.

• **Ultimate Questions**: the story covers some of the 'big questions' such as life after death/heaven and hell, good and evil, faith and doubt, suffering.

• **Pupils' World Views**: the story can help pupils clarify their own views on commitments and values for their own lives and life in general. Different characters/ symbolism could be the inspiration for discussion – e.g. Christian and Faithful at Vanity Fair – what would they do in response to a similar situation? Palace Beautiful/ fellowship – what does community mean to them and is it important for the 21st century?

Left:
Map of Bedford
in 1610.

HISTORY/
LOCAL HISTORY

The Pilgrim's Progress can be studied within the History curriculum using either the stimulus of the English Civil War/Stuart period as the main theme or the life of John Bunyan. A range of key skills in History can be covered, including: chronology, fact/opinion, similarities and differences, primary and secondary sources, empathy, historical enquiry, research and independent project work. For schools in Bedford and Bedfordshire a study of Bunyan is particularly relevant and allows for some excellent local History studies and 'Learning Outside the Classroom' opportunities.

Left:
Bunyan's House in
St Cuthbert's Street,
Bedford.

CREATIVE CURRICULUM

Using John Bunyan and *The Pilgrim's Progress* as the stimulus, a wide range of subjects, skills and activities can be covered by any year group or key stage for the duration of a week/fortnight or a full term. It is also possible for this to be a Creative Curriculum for the whole school, with key stages/classes covering different activities or the same activities at appropriate levels. A 'Creative Curriculum' map is included in this *Curriculum*.

This map is not exhaustive but is comprehensive and offers a wide range of suggestions for activities and skills work in the following curriculum areas:

• HISTORY, INCLUDING
  LOCAL HISTORY

• GEOGRAPHY

• RELIGIOUS EDUCATION

• LITERACY

• DRAMA

• MUSIC

• ART

• PHSE/SMSC

• LEARNING OUTSIDE
  THE CLASSROOM

• EXTENSION/ENRICHMENT

There are a number of additional resources available for teaching Bunyan and *The Pilgrim's Progress* as part of a Creative Curriculum. Details of these can be found on the 'Resources' page later in this *Curriculum* (see Chapter 4, p.75). Resources include a Teachers' Pack which contains supporting information on Bunyan's life and times and a variety of activity sheets/ ideas. Also available are images of the stained glass windows in Bunyan Meeting which depict scenes from the story, a map of Old Bedfordshire, adaptations of *The Pilgrim's Progress* on DVD/CD, a drama/documentary on the life of John Bunyan available on DVD, and a range of literature including a variety of children's editions of *The Pilgrim's Progress*. The John Bunyan Museum also offers Outreach Days in schools which could complement and enrich a Creative Curriculum programme of study.

Did you know?

Bunyan's world-famous hymn, *Who Would True Valour See*, is taken from verses Bunyan wrote for *The Pilgrim's Progress: Part II*. Singing in church was not common during Bunyan's time so it is unlikely these verses were originally written for use as a hymn.

> I have enjoyed studying *The Pilgrim's Progress* because it is interesting and fun. I enjoyed listening to *The Pilgrim's Progress* just being read to us. I will remember that the characters never gave up and always looked on the bright side of things.

Did you know?

Extracts from *The Pilgrim's Progress* and *The Pilgrim's Progress: Part II* have been used in funeral services of some famous people, including Queen Elizabeth The Queen Mother, Margaret Thatcher, the UK's first woman Prime Minister and Winston Churchill, British Prime Minister during World War II.

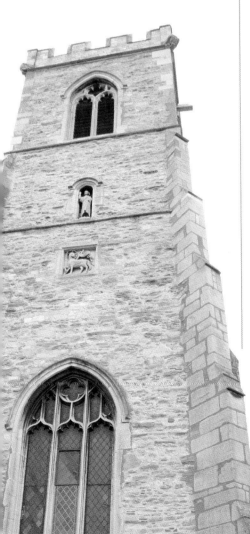

LEARNING OUTSIDE THE CLASSROOM

The Pilgrim's Progress also allows for a variety of opportunities relating to 'Learning Outside the Classroom'. For schools close enough Bunyan Meeting and the John Bunyan Museum in Bedford provide an excellent enrichment experience (see Week Nine of the suggested 'Religious Education: Scheme of Work' and the 'Bunyan Meeting/John Bunyan Museum' information page). Other suggestions include:

- Sites associated with Bunyan's life – Bedford/around Bedfordshire

- Bunyan Meeting and the John Bunyan Museum

- Theatre productions of *The Pilgrim's Progress*

- Stained glass windows depicting scenes from Bunyan's works (Bedford/Elstow/London)

- Civil War sites/museums

- Oliver Cromwell's house, Ely.

These are also listed in the 'Learning Outside the Classroom' section of the Creative Curriculum .

EXTENSION/ ENRICHMENT

There are a number of opportunities for extension and enrichment, of which just a few are suggested here:

- Project/research work: a host of topics are possible for project/ research work by pupils, depending on individual/class interests. This is an excellent method of enabling both extension and enrichment. Links with the John Bunyan Museum and/or local universities and other relevant organisations are worth exploring.

- Outreach days via the John Bunyan Museum. See website www.bunyanmeeting.co.uk

- Reading the original text. This enables pupils to explore the complete version of the story (including part II), study characters and symbolism in greater depth, and experience 17th century language/phrases.

For further resource information/ ideas, visit www.palacebeautiful.co.uk

Left:
St. John's Church, Bedford.

Did you know?

The Pilgrim's Progress introduces the reader to over 100 different characters, all symbolic of people we might meet on our (particularly spiritual) journey through life.

24

Using the Curriculum:

A guide to The Story Explained sections,
Scheme of Work, Outcomes, Creative
Curriculum and Glossary

> " I like the book and learning about John Bunyan's lifetime and the lessons are fun. The part I enjoy the most is from *The Pilgrim's Progress* where the pilgrims meet Pope and Pagan by the river. I didn't not enjoy anything because the lessons were very good. At the church I enjoyed going around and learning about the history. In the museum I liked seeing the images on the wall of the journey. The thing I will remember the most is the River of Death.

The Family Pilgrim's Progress by Jean Watson is the children's edition I have used in writing this *Curriculum*. This is the edition I choose to use when working with children, although all those listed on the 'Resources' page are editions I have used in the classroom and which work well. For the purposes of this *Curriculum* I have used the eleven chapters in *The Family Pilgrim's Progress* and condensed them into ten 'Story Explained' sections. This enables the story to fit into a ten week scheme focusing on one section per week of the story, as one approach to teaching the whole story. This approach would work particularly well when using it for whole school/class assembly time, or when teaching it as Literacy or Literacy/RE combined.

Alternatively, the suggested ten week 'Religious Education: Scheme of Work' included in this *Curriculum* covers the whole story and requires teachers to read the whole book and all ten 'Story Explained' sections for necessary background (as directed within the scheme) but uses only seven of the eleven chapters in class. This allows for an introductory session on John Bunyan and the setting for *The Pilgrim's Progress*, a 'Learning Outside the Classroom' activity (this could be adapted to a creative activity within school) and some consolidation of key concepts, within the ten week programme.

Above: Christian climbs the Hill Difficulty.

This Hill, though high, I covet to ascend,
The difficulty will not me offend:
For I perceive the way to life lies here;
Come, pluck up, Heart; let's neither faint nor fear:
Better, though difficult, the right way to go,
Than wrong, though easy, where the end is woe.

The Story Explained sections

The ten 'Story Explained' sections are listed below with the appropriate chapter references from *The Family Pilgrim's Progress* by Jean Watson. I have given each story section an appropriate title relating to a key Christian concept/s explored in that section of the story.

Story Section 1: The Book and the Burden

Chapter 1 – The Book

Story Section 2: The Wicket Gate

Chapter 2 – The Gate

Story Section 3: The Cross

Chapter 3 – The Cross

Story Section 4: Apollyon

Chapter 4 – The Fight

Story Section 5: The Valley of the Shadow of Death

Chapter 5 – Faithful

Story Section 6: Vanity Fair

Chapter 6 – Vanity Fair

Story Section 7: Faith, Hope, Love

Chapter 7 – Hopeful

Story Section 8: Faith and Doubt

Chapter 8 – Doubting Castle

Story Section 9: Knowledge and Experience

Chapter 9 – The Mountains and
Chapter 10 – A Testing Time

Story Section 10: The Celestial City

Chapter 10 – The City

Use of colour coding in text

The following colour coding has been used for ease of reference. This continues throughout the 'Religious Education: Suggested Scheme of Work', 'Outcomes' and 'Glossary' sections:

RED Characters names from *The Pilgrim's Progress*

GREEN Symbolic objects and places found in *The Pilgrim's Progress*

BLUE Key Christian words/concepts

BOLD Bible verses/references

With regard to Bible references, whilst John Bunyan would have used the Authorised Version in the main, the New International Version is used in this *Curriculum* as the language is more accessible. However, on a few occasions I have used the Authorised Version when the wording best reflects the meaning in relation to the identified symbolism or concept. Where I have used the Authorised Version, this is indicated by (AV) after the verse. Where I have referenced a whole section/ chapter, a key verse/s from this chapter will usually be quoted, in which case the verse number is given after the verse itself.

Please note: I have tried where possible to use terminology that is general rather than gender specific as characters from Bunyan's allegory can be symbolic of either male or female. However, as Bunyan has portrayed his characters as a particular gender and many of them (particularly the main characters – Christian, Faithful and Hopeful) as male, there may be times when I have had to use gender specific language.

I enjoyed studying *The Pilgrim's Progress* because we got to act, write questions, listen to the book and watch the story. The bit I enjoyed the most was when he had to battle Apollyon. But the bit I didn't like the best was when Faithful died at Vanity Fair and got burned by fire… I will remember most about John Bunyan when he wrote *The Pilgrim's Progress* in prison.

Summary

A summary of the story so far, with key characters in red, symbolism in green and Christian concepts in blue.

Christian Concepts

A list of Christian concepts covered in that section with a simple definition for each. These are also listed alphabetically in the 'Glossary' (see Chapter 3).

Key Characters and Symbolism

A list of the key characters/symbolism with a brief explanation of each and how they link to the story, the Bible and the Christian faith.

Bunyan's 'Real-Life' Inspiration

Information on Bunyan's real-life inspiration, where relevant. Knowledge of Bunyan's personal, real-life inspiration for *The Pilgrim's Progress* helps to bring the man and his story to life. Imaginations can also be fired by discussions/research into possible alternative 'real-life inspirations' from your own local history and environs.

Related Bible Verses and Texts

Bible verses relating to the symbolism and relevant Christian concepts. These are just some examples of Bible teaching/references in relation to each. Many more can be found in both the Old and New Testaments – an excellent extension/ enrichment activity (for example, children could research texts on light, heaven, wisdom, angels, etc).

Religious Education: Suggested Scheme of Work
KS1, Lower KS2, Upper KS2

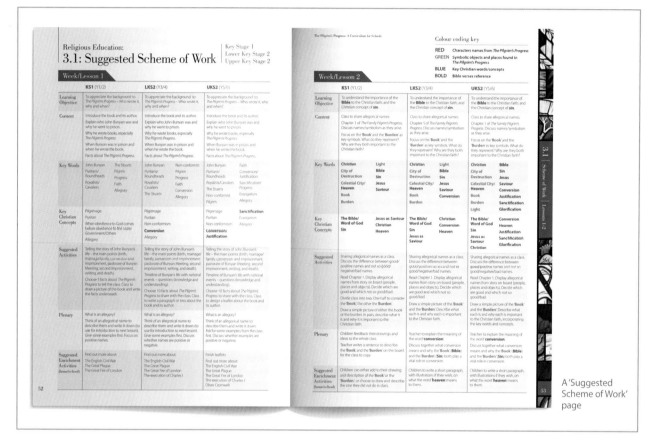

A 'Suggested Scheme of Work' page

The ten week 'Religious Education: Scheme of Work' that follows covers the whole story but uses only seven of the 'Story Explained' sections directly for class work (sections 1, 2, 3, 4, 6, 8 and 10). It is, of course, important that the missing sections/chapters are read and understood by teachers and a brief summary given to classes before commencing the next stage of the story. The additional three weeks of the ten week scheme cover:

- A brief introduction to John Bunyan – his life and times (Week One)

- 'Learning Outside the Classroom' – a trip to Bunyan Meeting and the John Bunyan Museum (Week Nine)

- A consolidation of key concepts learnt (Week Ten).

Schools may prefer to use the full ten weeks for the story, in which case each 'Story Explained' section with related chapters should be followed. Background to John Bunyan, his life and times, could be taught alongside the story.

The scheme suggests that chapters be read to the class as the medium for presenting the story. Pupils really enjoy listening to it and it allows for explanation/discussion as you read – particularly useful given Bunyan's extensive use of symbolism. Teachers may prefer to vary this by using media adaptations for some chapters/sections or, if time allows, using both; or involve children themselves in the reading. There are two film adaptations listed on the 'Resources' page and both fit well with any of the children's editions

listed in this *Curriculum*. Varying the presentation medium also allows for discussion on the effectiveness of each and why.

Key words and key Christian concepts for each lesson are listed, all colour-coded within the scheme for ease of reference. These are the words/concepts that particularly relate to the learning objective/s for that lesson. The ten 'Story Explained' sections will have explanations for these and the 'Glossary' at the end of this *Curriculum* gives the definitions of key Christian words/concepts covered in the whole story in alphabetical order. Bible verses listed in the 'Story Explained' sections demonstrate how everything Bunyan wrote was inspired by the Bible. Many of these verses are either used within or referenced alongside Bunyan's

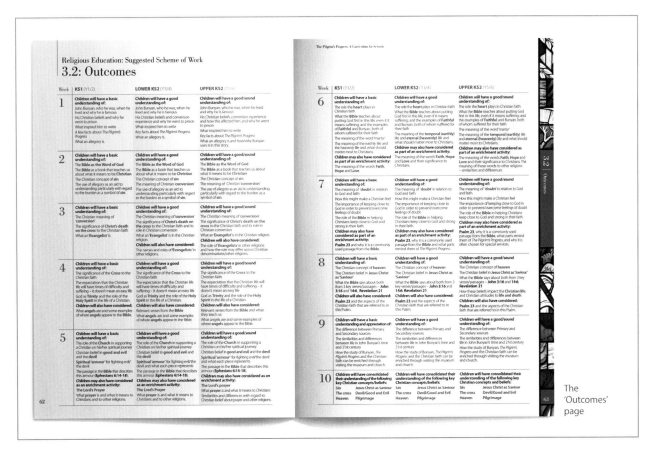

The 'Outcomes' page

Did you know?

The title *The Pilgrim's Progress* generally refers to the story of Christian's journey to the Celestial City, first published in 1678. *The Pilgrim's Progress: Part II* was published in 1684, with a second edition in 1686. It is less well-known and not always included in publications of Bunyan's *The Pilgrim's Progress*.

original text. The scheme then gives ideas for activities within class which teachers may follow or adapt, as appropriate. The ideas listed in the 'Suggested Enrichment Activities' section are ideas for activities/research that could be done at home or at school in pupils' own time. (When pupils are well-motivated they are often keen to do more in their own time voluntarily and so to encourage this I have chosen not to call this section 'homework').

The activities suggested in this scheme are designed to be progressive from KS1 through to Upper KS2 (from 5 years of age to 11 years of age) and are planned to support differentiation and attainment by outcome. Where activities are very similar, differentiation should be promoted through depth of conversation/discussion on key concepts and related activity outcomes.

The 'Outcomes' section which follows the ten week scheme summarises weekly learning outcomes, providing an 'at a glance' overview of learning outcomes. This is designed to be a useful tool for classroom and subject teachers, also supply teachers, teaching assistants and others working with/alongside the teacher and pupils. It can also help schools when planning programmes of study for year groups/key stages to ensure coverage of key Christian concepts. Assessment is not covered as there is now increasing diversity amongst schools with regard to chosen assessment procedures and terminology. Depending on how this *Curriculum* is used, schools may want to devise a more detailed and personalised outcomes/assessment tool for *The Pilgrim's Progress* in line with individual school assessment policies or

you may not need anything more than what is provided here. Not all learning opportunities need to be formally assessed; indeed some have more impact when they are not!

The study of *The Pilgrim's Progress* and the life and times of its author John Bunyan provides many opportunities for extension and enrichment. The 'Creative Curriculum' map included in this *Curriculum* can be used alongside the 'Religious Education: Suggested Scheme of Work' for ideas to extend and enrich the learning for pupils who want/are able to study deeper and/or wider, or it can be used as a curriculum in its own right (see also 'Using *The Pilgrim's Progress* in School').

Did you know?

There were three editions of *The Pilgrim's Progress* in the space of one year (1678-9).

Chapter 2
The Story Explained...

CHRISTIAN·APPROACHES·THE·HOUSE·BEAUTIFUL

Where am I now? Is this the love and care
Of Jesus, for the men that pilgrims are?
Thus to provide! That I should be forgiven!
And dwell already the next door to heaven.

The Story Explained...
2.1: The Book and the Burden

Summary

This chapter introduces us to the central character, **CHRISTIAN**. *The Pilgrim's Progress* is the story of Christian's journey from his home town, the **CITY OF DESTRUCTION**, to the **CELESTIAL CITY** (**HEAVEN**). Christian lives in the City of Destruction with his wife **CHRISTIANA AND THEIR FOUR CHILDREN**. One day he finds an old Bible in his attic and begins to read it. He begins to be aware of his own sinfulness and imperfection in the sight of God and becomes increasingly troubled. A '**GREAT BURDEN**' grows on his back, a symbol of his sin and his awareness of it. Christian meets **EVANGELIST**, who helps to make sense of things and guides Christian towards '**THE LIGHT**' and the '**WICKET-GATE**'. Christian wants his family to come with him but knows he will never persuade them, so, knowing God must come first in everything, Christian sets out alone. Two of his neighbours chase after him. Living up to their names, **OBSTINATE** refuses to join him, whilst **PLIABLE** is easily persuaded.

Key Characters and Symbolism

CHRISTIAN: Formerly called **GRACELESS**. Both names are symbolic of his spiritual state before God. As 'Graceless' he knew nothing of the **GRACE** of God in sending his son, Jesus Christ, as a sacrifice in order that believers may inherit eternal life. *The Pilgrim's Progress* (Christian is the pilgrim) tells the story of a pilgrim's journey from **SIN** to **SALVATION** through the Christian concepts of **JUSTIFICATION**, **SANCTIFICATION** and **GLORIFICATION**.

EVANGELIST: Symbolic of a Puritan minister/preacher. This character is based on John Bunyan's own first pastor and spiritual guide, the 'holy Mr Gifford' of St. John's Church, Bedford. Evangelist points Christian in the right direction – towards Christ.

CHRISTIANA and THE CHILDREN: Christian's wife and family. In *The Pilgrim's Progress* they refuse to listen to Christian and think he is misguided. But Christian, desperately sad at having to leave them, continues to pray for them and eventually they too make the journey from the City of Destruction to the Celestial City. Their journey is told in *The Pilgrim's Progress: Part II*.

OBSTINATE and **PLIABLE**: Two characters Christian meets on his way. Their names are symbolic of their characters. One is too stubborn to listen whilst the other has no stamina for the journey and gives in when the going gets tough.

CITY OF DESTRUCTION: Symbolic of the world without God.

CELESTIAL CITY: **HEAVEN**.

BURDEN: Symbolic of **SIN** and the pilgrim's growing conviction of it.

BOOK: The **BIBLE/WORD of GOD**. This is the most valuable spiritual guide for Christians.

LIGHT: Symbolic of the Word of God and also of Jesus Christ who is described in the Bible as '**THE LIGHT OF THE WORLD**'.

WICKET-GATE: Symbolic of the moment when a person becomes a true believer – more typically described as '**CONVERSION**'. It is Christ who works in a person to enable him/her to enter through the 'Wicket-gate'.

Related Bible Verses and Texts

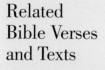

Psalm 38:4 'My guilt has overwhelmed me like a burden too heavy to bear' (**Sin/Burden**)

Matthew 3:7 'Flee from the wrath to come' (AV) (**Hell**)

Matthew 7:8 '…and to the one who knocks, the door will be opened.' (**Christ/Wicket-gate**)

Psalm 119:105 'Your word is a lamp for my feet and a light on my path' (**Word of God/Light**)

John 8:12 'I am the light of the world. Whoever follows me will never walk in darkness, but will have the light of life.' (**Christ/Light**)

Matthew 7:13-14 'Enter through the narrow gate. For wide is the gate and broad is the road that leads to destruction, and many enter through it. But small is the gate and narrow the road that leads to life, and only a few find it.' (**Conversion/Wicket-gate**)

Matthew 13 *The Parable of the Sower* 'But since they have no root, they last only a short time. When trouble or persecution comes because of the word, they quickly fall away.' (v.21) (**Pliable**)

Colour coding key

RED	Characters names from *The Pilgrim's Progress*
GREEN	Symbolic objects and places found in *The Pilgrim's Progress*
BLUE	Key Christian words/concepts
BOLD	Bible verses/references

Christian Concepts

GOD: Our Creator. In Christian belief God is **TRINITY** (three in one): God the Father, God the Son (Jesus Christ) and God the Holy Spirit.

SIN: This word describes the wrong things we do, but also our imperfection generally. The Bible teaches that however good we are or try to be we will never match the perfection and purity of our creator God. Bunyan describes this as 'God with reference to us'.

SALVATION: The saving of the soul through deliverance from sin and its consequences by the death of Christ on the cross.

GRACE: Describes Christ's sacrifice on the cross and the forgiveness of sins for all true believers.

HEAVEN and HELL: Heaven is an eternity with Christ. Hell is an eternity without, likened in the Bible to a 'lake of fire'.

The WORD of GOD: The Bible, made up of 66 books, divided into The Old Testament and the New Testament. The Bible is the word of God handed down for people to learn about God and how to grow in faith.

CHRIST, LIGHT of THE WORLD: In the Bible Christ is likened to a 'light' because through him it is possible to see life more clearly. It is Christ that helps direct the journey of life for a believer, much like a lamp/light helps us see in the dark.

CONVERSION: Becoming Christian. Symbolised in *The Pilgrim's Progress* as both a process (Christian) and an instantaneous experience (Hopeful).

JUSTIFICATION: Conversion means receiving the grace of God in sending his Son to die on the cross. When this grace is received, sins are forgiven and the believer is justified in the sight of God and receives the promise of eternal life.

SANCTIFICATION: Sanctification means the Christian pilgrimage, or journey, of faith. As believers progress in faith, keep close to Christ and desire to be like him, they are gradually being sanctified. The larger part of *The Pilgrims' Progress* is describing Christian's journey of sanctification.

GLORIFICATION: The realisation of the promise of eternal life, the moment when believers enter heaven and are glorified with Christ. This was Christian's ultimate goal – his safe arrival at the Celestial City.

Symbolism: Bunyan's 'Real-Life' Inspiration

CHRISTIAN	Much of the main character Christian is believed to have been inspired by Bunyan's own life and experiences – hence the reason why the stained glass windows in Bunyan Meeting depict Christian as Bunyan. For example, Bunyan's own conversion experience was more of a process – it took many years for him to get from the Wicket-gate to the cross. But Bunyan would also have incorporated characteristics and experiences of others in developing the character Christian.
EVANGELIST	The inspiration for this character was the Rev. John Gifford, first pastor of St. John's Church, Bedford and Bunyan's first real spiritual guide and mentor. It was 'the holy Mr Gifford' as Bunyan called him, who directed Bunyan towards Christ and the cross.
CITY of DESTRUCTION	Bunyan would have been thinking of the state of his country as well as his own community and their need for God and salvation when describing the City of Destruction.
BURDEN	Christian's burden is said to be inspired by the anvil that Bunyan used to carry around with him in his work as a tinker. The anvil would have been very heavy and a constant 'burden' to Bunyan as he travelled around the local villages.
THE WICKET-GATE	An old oak door to the left of the main doorway of the parish church at Elstow is believed to be the inspiration for the Wicket-gate. This was the church where Bunyan was baptised as a new-born baby, the church he attended as a teenager and the church where he heard the sermon by the Rev. Christopher Hall on the sin of playing sports on the Sabbath – a sermon that was to have a profound effect on the young John Bunyan (see biography in Chapter 1).

The Story Explained...
2.2: The Wicket-Gate

Summary

CHRISTIAN and PLIABLE continue journeying towards the light. At this point Pliable is very eager but has not grown his own burden – a sign that he has no sense of his own sinfulness in relation to God. So, when they fall into the SLOUGH of DESPOND, Pliable loses interest and gets out easily (because he has no burden or awareness of sin). Christian struggles to get out until he is offered a helping hand by a character called HELP, who tells him of the STEPS that are there to help them through the Slough. Christian, being a new pilgrim and not yet 'Christian', has little knowledge of God's promises at this stage in his journey and so is not able to see or use the steps himself – he needs 'Help' to get out.

Once on his way again he meets WORLDLY-WISEMAN who understands all about his burden. He directs him to the VILLAGE of MORALITY via a HILL, to a man named LEGALITY who will help release him of his burden. He is very convincing, so Christian decides to follow his directions and head for the village. Unfortunately, Christian has been given bad advice and he finds himself passing under a ridge and flames spurting out of the hill. It is at this point that he realises his mistake.

EVANGELIST appears. He tells Christian off for straying from God's way and then explains why it is the wrong way – the LAW can never set us free from the burden of sin, only the CROSS can do that. Evangelist directs Christian back to the right path.

Christian soon reaches the WICKET-GATE and is pulled through by GOODWILL, the gatekeeper, who warns him of the dangers of CAPTAIN BEELZEBUB. Goodwill points him in the direction of the STRAIGHT and NARROW PATH which will lead him to a house owned by the INTERPRETER.

Key Characters and Symbolism

CHRISTIAN: Not yet 'Christian' and still carrying his burden.

PLIABLE: (see 'Story Section'1)

HELP: A symbol of the 'helps' (GOD's PROMISES, found in Bible verses and texts) true believers are given along the way.

WORLDLY-WISEMAN: Represents a dependence on moral behaviour/good works as directed by the OLD TESTAMENT LAW (see Exodus 20:1-21, The Ten Commandments).

LEGALITY: Symbolising the Old Testament law.

EVANGELIST: Spiritual guide. A very important role in the Christian pilgrimage. As true pilgrims make progress in their journey they mature in their faith and may not need so much support as they do at the beginning. Christian is not yet 'Christian' and therefore is very dependent on Evangelist to explain and direct him in matters of a spiritual nature.

GOODWILL: This is Christ, who works in the believer to bring him through the Wicket-gate into true belief and Christian pilgrimage.

CAPTAIN BEELZEBUB: The DEVIL, the enemy of God and his people, who works hard to prevent pilgrims becoming Christian and continues to battle with them in varying degrees along the way.

The INTERPRETER: The HOLY SPIRIT, who helps the believer to grow in knowledge and faith. Spiritual guides, such as Evangelist, help believers to interpret God's word, so aiding the work of the Holy Spirit.

SLOUGH OF DESPOND: Symbolises the awareness/conviction of all that is bad and sinful individually as well as universally, before a pilgrim becomes Christian. It will always exist as there will always be sin in the world as it is.

STEPS: God's promises – assurances of salvation by faith through the cross. Christian has yet to experience the cross so does not see the steps.

VILLAGE called MORALITY: Symbolises the attempt to achieve salvation through good works and the law.

The HILL: The Hill and the flames coming out of it are symbolic of humanity's futile attempts to become Christian by good works (the LAW/morality). The Bible teaches that our best attempts will never be good enough as we are all imperfect, hence the reason why Christian's burden feels greater the more he is aware of and tries to follow the law. The only way to God (and to lose his burden) is through Christ who dealt with sin at the cross (GRACE).

WICKET-GATE: Symbolises the point of conversion.

STRAIGHT and NARROW PATH: The Bible teaches that the way to heaven is not easy – it is 'straight' and 'narrow'.

Related Bible Verses and Texts

1 John 4:1-6 'They are from the world and therefore speak from the viewpoint of the world, and the world listens to them'. (v.5) (**Worldly-Wiseman**)

Romans 6:14 'For sin shall no longer be your master, because you are not under the law, but under grace.' (**Legality/Village called Morality**)

Galatians 3:10 'Cursed is everyone who does not continue to do everything written in the book of the law.' (**Hill**)

John 6:37 and 40 'All those the Father gives me will come to me, and whoever comes to me I will never drive away'; 'For my Father's will is that everyone who looks to the Son and believes in him shall have eternal life, and I will raise them up at the last day'. (**Wicket-gate**)

Luke 13:24 'Make every effort to enter through the narrow door, because many, I tell you, will try to enter and will not be able to'. (**Wicket-gate/straight and narrow path**)

Ephesians 1:13 'And you also were included in Christ when you heard the message of truth, the gospel of your salvation. When you believed, you were marked in him with a seal, the promised Holy Spirit.' (**Interpreter/Holy Spirit**)

Christian Concepts

GOD'S PROMISES: Verses in the Bible that assure the Christian of salvation by faith. The better believers know and understand the Bible the more they are able to call upon these promises in times of trouble.

The OLD TESTAMENT LAW: The law given by God to Moses (includes the Ten Commandments, see **Exodus 20:1-21**) This was the Old Covenant between God and his people to help direct them live good lives and honour God. With the coming of the New Covenant (Christ/Grace) the need for the Old Covenant was abolished, although it is still a useful guide.

GRACE: Describes Christ's sacrifice on the cross and the forgiveness of sins for all true believers.

The DEVIL: A fallen angel who is the enemy of God and his people. Also known in the Bible as **SATAN** and **APOLLYON**.

The HOLY SPIRIT: Part of God as **TRINITY**. The Holy Spirit lives in all true believers and acts as spiritual guide, interpreter and helper.

Symbolism: Bunyan's 'Real-Life' Inspiration

WORLDLY WISEMAN	Possibly inspired by Edward Fowler, Rector of Northill, Bedfordshire, who advocated good works as a means to salvation. Bunyan attacked these views in *A Defence of the Doctrine of Justification by Faith* (1672).
SLOUGH of DESPOND	A possible inspiration for the Slough of Despond is the area between Bunyan's birthplace in Harrowden and Elstow Village. In the 17th century this would have been marshy ground.
The HILL	In his book *Grace Abounding* Bunyan describes how, before he became a Christian, he feared that the tower of the parish church at Elstow where he was a bell-ringer would fall on his head as punishment for his sins. Eventually he gave up both ringing the bells and watching them being rung, for fear that he would be punished in this way.
CAPTAIN BEELZEBUB'S CASTLE	Believed to have been inspired by the bell tower of the parish church at Elstow.

The Story Explained...
2.3: The Cross

Summary

CHRISTIAN arrives at the House of the INTERPRETER. Here he is instructed in important spiritual truths via a series of emblems, pictures and tableaux, such as PASSION and PATIENCE, BACKSLIDER and UNREADY. After receiving this instruction, Christian is ready to continue his journey to the cross.

He comes to a simple rough track with a wall either side – the WALL of SALVATION. At the top of the hill is the CROSS with an open grave at the foot of it. Here the BURDEN easily falls from Christian's shoulders and rolls into the open grave, never to be seen again. It is here that Christian experiences the ASSURANCE of salvation and is overcome with emotion. THREE ANGELS appear to give him marks that symbolise this assurance: they tell him his sins are forgiven, give him clean clothes (he would have been dressed in rags), a mark on his forehead, a KEY of PROMISE and a SCROLL. Christian now experiences a feeling of freedom for the first time. His burden is gone and he knows his salvation is secure. He weeps tears of joy and goes on his way, praising God.

At the end of the valley is a very steep hill – the HILL DIFFICULTY. This is symbolic of the Christian life, what Bunyan describes in the original text as a 'desperate journey'. The Bible says there will be suffering along the way as well as much peace and joy. But God gives us many 'Helps', signs of his continuing GRACE to believers. At the bottom of the Hill is a SPRING of WATER to help true pilgrims ascend the hill.

Half way up Christian spies a BENCH where he can rest. But he makes the mistake of falling asleep and dropping his scroll, which rolls under the Bench.

Key Characters and Symbolism

CHRISTIAN: Now a true 'CHRISTIAN' as he has entered through the Wicket-gate and experienced regeneration, a new birth in Christ. But he carries his burden until he gets to the cross because he has not yet experienced ASSURANCE of his salvation.

The INTERPRETER: Symbolic of the HOLY SPIRIT; teaches Christian important spiritual truths.

PASSION and PATIENCE: Symbolic of two types of people: those chasing earthly pleasures that can be had now (Passion); and those on pilgrimage to heaven who are content to wait for eternal glory (Patience).

BACKSLIDER: The Man in an Iron Cage, who has stepped off the right road and wandered where he pleased. The iron cage is symbolic of his despair and inability to find his way back.

UNREADY: A man terrified by the thoughts of JUDGEMENT DAY because he is not ready to face his maker, God.

The THREE ANGELS: Sent from God to Christian when he arrives at the cross. From them he receives assurance of his salvation. He is told his sins are forgiven, he is given a change of clothes, a mark on his forehead, the Key of Promise and a Scroll.

WALL of SALVATION: Two thick walls that border the path leading up to the cross.

BURDEN: Symbolic of sin. Christian loses his burden at the cross. In *The Pilgrim's Progress* Christian is the only character that we see carrying a burden. This is because Bunyan wanted his readers to identify with Christian and understand what it is like to become 'Christian'. When Christian loses his burden we are told that he never sees it again. Bunyan wanted his readers to know that to become 'Christian' means having sins forgiven and the assurance of salvation. The burden is seen no more.

KEY of PROMISE: Another symbol of God's promises, given in the Bible.

SCROLL: A symbol of the assurance of salvation by faith and a guide to help Christians on their way. At the end of the story, Christian and his companion Hopeful hand in their Scrolls to gain entrance to heaven. (The character IGNORANCE does not have such a Scroll and so, in the final scene of the story in the original version, he is denied entrance and taken off to hell. See story section 2:10)

HILL DIFFICULTY: Symbolic of the trials and the suffering the Christian will experience on his journey through life.

SPRING of WATER: Water is often referred to in the Bible as symbolic of Christ and the life offered through his death on the cross. Here it is symbolic of another of the 'Helps' for pilgrims. (See John 4)

BENCH: Another of the 'Helps' that pilgrims are offered. Meant for resting. But it can also be misused, with pilgrims falling asleep. Christians should never fall (spiritually) asleep.

Did you know?

The Pilgrim's Progress: Part II tells the story of Christian's wife, Christiana, her four boys and her friend, Mercy, as they follow Christian from the City of Destruction to the Celestial City.

Related Bible Verses and Texts

John 14:26 'But the Counsellor, the Holy Spirit, whom the Father will send in my name, will teach you all things and will remind you of everything I have said to you.' (**Interpreter/Holy Spirit**)

Galations 5:22-24 'But the fruit of the Spirit is love, joy, peace, forbearance, kindness, goodness, faithfulness, gentleness and self-control. Against such things there is no law. Those who belong to Christ Jesus have crucified the flesh with its passions and desires.' (**Passion and Patience**)

John 3:16 'For God so loved the world that he gave his one and only Son, that whoever believes in him shall not perish but have eternal life.'

John 14:6 'Jesus said to him, 'I am the way, and the truth, and the life. No one comes to the Father except through me.' (**Cross/Salvation**)

Acts 14:22 'We must go through many hardships to enter the Kingdom of God.' (**Hill Difficulty**)

John 4:14 'But whoever drinks the water I give them will never thirst. Indeed, the water I give them will become in them a spring of water welling up to eternal life.' (**Spring of Water**)

Exodus 3:1-6, Psalm 91:11, Luke 15:10, Luke 1:26-38, John 20:12 (**Angels**)

Christian Concepts

CHRISTIAN: The name given to a person who believes that Jesus Christ is the Son of God, has asked forgiveness for sin and who has experienced conversion into a new life in Christ. For some the experience of conversion and the cross/assurance happens at the same time; for others, such as Bunyan and Christian here, conversion is more of a process over time.

HOLY SPIRIT: Part of the **TRINITY**. The Holy Spirit lives in all true believers and acts as spiritual guide, interpreter and helper.

JUDGEMENT DAY: The Bible teaches that all will be judged at the end of time (see **John 5:28-30** and **Revelation 20:11-13**)

The CROSS: Christ died on the cross in order that we might be forgiven for our sin. The Bible teaches that Christ is the only way to God. Christ's death and Resurrection is celebrated by Christians at Easter and is the pivotal doctrine of Christianity.

ASSURANCE: The certainty of a salvation that will not be taken away.

ETERNAL LIFE/HEAVEN: Christians are promised eternal life with God in heaven. Christian's focus is on the Celestial City – things eternal (heavenly) not temporal (earthly).

ANGELS: Divine beings. There are good angels and fallen angels. The Bible teaches that God sends angels to watch over us (see **Psalm 91:11**).

Symbolism: Bunyan's 'Real-Life' Inspiration

CHRISTIAN	In Christian, Bunyan is reflecting his own process of conversion. Even after Bunyan had received forgiveness for his sins and become 'Christian' he was unable to forgive himself and for a number of years he did not have the assurance that comes with conversion. The freedom and the emotion that Bunyan himself felt when he finally experienced the cross are described here in the scene where Christian arrives at the cross and his burden falls away.
INTERPRETER and INTERPRETER'S HOUSE	John Gifford and his home, the rectory of St. John's Church, Bedford, are believed to be the inspiration for Interpreter and Interpreter's House. Gifford was the first pastor of Bunyan Meeting and much valued by Bunyan as spiritual guide and mentor in the early days of his Christian journey.
UNREADY	Inspired by Bunyan's own 'fearful dreams' that he describes in his spiritual autobiography *Grace Abounding*.
HILL DIFFICULTY	Inspired by the hill range just north of the Georgian town of Ampthill, Bedfordshire. In Bunyan's time, the track from Bedford to Ampthill would have been steep and difficult.
CROSS	The cross and church well in the Bedfordshire village of Stevington may have been in Bunyan's mind as he wrote the scene at the cross.

The Story Explained...
2.4: Apollyon

Summary

Christian meets **MISTRUST** and **TIMOROUS**, two characters who are not interested in withstanding the challenges of the journey. They unsettle Christian who reaches for his scroll for comfort, only to realise he has lost it. In dismay, he has to retrace his steps, all the time admonishing himself for falling asleep.

He finds the scroll under the bench and determines not to lose it again. He continues his journey to the **PALACE BEAUTIFUL**. The entrance is guarded by two lions which initially put him off, but he discovers the lions are chained and stationed there to keep false pilgrims out. The Palace Beautiful is for true pilgrims only, a place of rest and refreshment. The Gate-keeper, **WATCHFUL**, introduces Christian to **DISCRETION**, **PIETY**, **PRUDENCE** and **CHARITY**, sisters who live at the Palace. They talk with Christian about his journey to establish that he is a true believer. Christian stays for a few days, sleeping in a room called **PEACE**. Whilst at the Palace Christian has time to renew his physical and spiritual strength and is given glimpses of the **DELECTABLE MOUNTAINS** and **IMMANUEL'S LAND** for additional encouragement.

Before leaving the Palace Christian is fitted with **ARMOUR** from head to foot – symbolic of the spiritual armour the Bible tells us about. The sisters walk with him to the bottom of the hill, sharing **BREAD** and **WINE** with him before he heads off alone.

In the **VALLEY of HUMBLING** Christian meets **APOLLYON** (the devil) and engages in a terrible fight with him. Christian is badly wounded but, using the **ARMOUR** that he has been given at the Palace – **the SHIELD of FAITH**, **the SWORD of the SPIRIT** and the **WORD of GOD** – he secures the victory. God provides **LEAVES** from the tree of life to heal Christian's wounds.

Key Characters and Symbolism

MISTRUST and **TIMOROUS**: Characters that live up to their names and leave the journey when it gets tough. They are not true pilgrims and do not carry burdens.

WATCHFUL: Along with the sisters, Watchful has an important role investigating whether pilgrims are true Christians. This is symbolic of the practice of the non-conformist church at that time – church membership was not an easy process.

DISCRETION: One of the sisters who welcomes Christian to the Palace. Her name reflects her character and role at the Palace.

PIETY and **PRUDENCE**: Sisters who help ensure Christian's stay at the Palace is spiritually and physically profitable. The names of the residents at the Palace reflect characteristics that were considered vital in non-conformist church life.

CHARITY: The biblical word for 'LOVE'.

APOLLYON: The Prince of the City of Destruction – the devil. The fight here symbolises the spiritual warfare that Christians will be engaged in during their lives, although not every Christian will experience such terrible warfare as Christian experiences here.

PALACE BEAUTIFUL: Symbolic of the non-conformist church, a place of spiritual and physical refreshment. Only true believers were admitted to membership to ensure that pilgrims experienced true peace, fellowship and spiritual growth and encouragement.

TWO LIONS: Symbolising the need to guard against false pilgrims entering the church.

A bedroom named PEACE: The name symbolises an important characteristic of the non-conformist church.

DELECTABLE MOUNTAINS and **IMMANUEL's LAND**: Beautiful land which borders heaven, where, with the help of the shepherds that live there, pilgrims can gain a distant view of the gate of the Celestial City.

ARMOUR: Symbolic of the **SPIRITUAL ARMOUR** described in **Ephesians 6:14-18**.

BREAD and WINE: Symbolic of **COMMUNION** (the Last Supper), which strengthens pilgrims and keeps them focused on Christ.

VALLEY of HUMBLING: Symbolic of times of conflict and trial, guarding us against spiritual pride and complacency.

LEAVES: Symbolic of leaves from the Tree of life, planted by God in the Garden of Eden.

Related Bible Verses and Texts

1 Corinthians 13:13 'And now these three remain: faith, hope and love. But the greatest of these is love.' (**Charity**)

Revelation 9:11 'They had as king over them the angel of the Abyss, whose name in Hebrew is Abaddon, and in Greek is Apollyon (that is, Destroyer).'

Romans 6:23 'For the wages of sin is death, but the gift of God is eternal life in Christ Jesus our Lord.'

James 4:7 'Submit yourselves, then, to God. Resist the devil, and he will flee from you.'

Romans 8:37 'No, in all these things we are more than conquerors through him who loved us.' (**Apollyon/Spiritual Warfare**)

Isaiah 33:16, 17 '…they are the ones who will dwell on the heights, whose refuge will be the mountain fortress. Their bread will be supplied, and water will not fail them. Your eyes will see the king in his beauty and view a land that stretches afar.' (**Delectable Mountains/Immanuel's Land**)

Ephesians 6:14-18 'Stand firm then, with the belt of truth buckled around your waist, with the breast plate of righteousness in place, and with your feet fitted with the readiness that comes from the gospel of peace. In addition to all this, take up the shield of faith, with which you can extinguish all the flaming arrows of the evil one. Take the helmet of salvation and the sword of the Spirit, which is the word of God.' (**Armour**)

Mark 14:12-26 The Lord's Supper. (**Bread and Wine/Communion**)

Genesis 2:9 'And the Lord God made all kinds of trees grow out of the ground – trees that were pleasing to the eye and good for food. In the middle of the garden were the tree of life and the tree of the knowledge of good and evil.' Also **Psalm 1:3** (**Leaves**).

Christian Concepts

The DEVIL/APOLLYON/SPIRITUAL WARFARE: The enemy of God, a fallen angel who desires the destruction of God's kingdom and the souls of humanity. The devil fights to keep believers and non-believers away from God. Although terrible, this spiritual warfare aids Christians in their spiritual growth. The devil is also called Captain Beelzebub by Bunyan.

SPIRITUAL ARMOUR: These are spiritual weapons for the protection of Christians and particularly for times of spiritual warfare (see **Ephesians 6**).

GOD'S SOVEREIGNTY: God is ultimately in control of everything. In the original version, Bunyan uses the phrase 'as God would have it' a number of times (including in the scene with Apollyon), portraying his belief that ultimately God is in control of events.

The LORD'S SUPPER/COMMUNION: The first Lord's Supper was shared by Christ with his twelve disciples just before he was arrested. The bread and the wine remind Christians of Jesus – his body and his blood.

Symbolism: Bunyan's 'Real-Life' Inspiration

DISCRETION, PIETY, PRUDENCE, CHARITY	Female characters possibly inspired by the poor women he overheard in Bedford talking of spiritual things (see Chapter 1: 'John Bunyan – a Brief Biography').
APOLLYON	The fight between Christian and Apollyon would have been inspired by the chapbooks Bunyan read in his youth which told stories of dragons, knights and giants in combat.
PALACE BEAUTIFUL	Represents the non-conformist church, possibly in part inspired by the independent church in Bedford which Bunyan attended. The Palace itself is inspired by Houghton House, a former Jacobean hunting-lodge at the top of Ampthill Hill built in 1621 and the stateliest building in the area in Bunyan's time. It is believed Bunyan visited Houghton House as a tinker to mend pots and pans. The main staircase from the House is now in the Swan Hotel, Bedford.
DELECTABLE MOUNTAINS and IMMANUEL'S LAND	Inspired by the Chiltern Hills, which on a clear day can be seen from Houghton House. Bunyan would have been familiar with these hills, preaching on many occasions in secret locations between Dunstable and Hitchin. Because Bunyan would not have travelled widely throughout the British Isles these hills would have appeared mountainous.

The Story Explained...
2.5: The Valley of the Shadow of Death

Summary

CHRISTIAN enters the **VALLEY of the SHADOW of DEATH**. He carries his **SWORD of the SPIRIT** (part of his spiritual armour) at all times, this time at the ready. The Valley is very dark, narrow and dangerous. Christian uses another spiritual weapon to help him through – **PRAYER**.

Christian hears the voice of another Christian who is reciting the words of **Psalm 23**. This is just what Christian needs to help him through the valley. When morning comes Christian can see more clearly the dangers in the valley. The second part of the valley is even more dangerous, but with the light Christian is able to see his way better. At the end of the valley he meets **FAITHFUL**, an old friend from the City of Destruction. He runs to catch up with him but in being too keen and quick he overtakes him and promptly falls over, reminding us of the popular proverb 'Pride comes before a fall' – the origins of which are found in the Bible (**Proverbs 16:18**).

Christian and Faithful exchange stories about their journeys. Faithful describes his encounters with the temptress **WANTON** and then, on the Hill Difficulty, **ADAM-THE-FIRST**, who tempts Faithful with his 3 daughters – **LUST of the FLESH**, **LUST of the EYES** and the **PRIDE of LIFE**. Faithful withstands the temptation but then meets a man who tells him off for being tempted and physically assaults him. When Faithful begs forgiveness the man says he doesn't know how to show mercy. This man is symbolic of **MOSES**, the law-giver, who only had the **LAW** to live by, not the **CROSS of CHRIST**. Faithful is then rescued by another man, who sends Moses away. This man is **CHRIST the SAVIOUR**.

Faithful, we are told, then walked past the Palace Beautiful because he was keen to progress with his journey. He tells Christian of his meetings with **DISCONTENT** (who tries to make him discontented with his progress and his faith) and **SHAME** (a character symbolic of people who are ashamed of their faith, preferring to talk it down rather than defend it). Christian then shares his experience of his encounter with Apollyon.

Their conversation and friendship demonstrate the importance for Christians of sharing spiritual experiences with fellow pilgrims. **FELLOWSHIP** with other Christians is another way of making progress in faith and wisdom and enables Christians to give and receive support.

Key Characters and Symbolism

FAITHFUL: His name is symbolic of his character, as we will see as the story progresses. **FAITH** is one of the three theological virtues as defined by St. Paul (the others being **HOPE** and **LOVE**). Faithful is also symbolic of Christian companionship/fellowship – he is the first of two pilgrims who journey with Christian as friend and companion (the other is **HOPEFUL** who we meet later).

WANTON: Tempted Faithful with her beauty, an example of the temptations/distractions of this world.

ADAM the FIRST: Symbolic of the first Adam who represents sin and the corruption of the world.

LUST of the FLESH, **LUST of the EYES**, **PRIDE of LIFE**: Names are symbolic of their characters and the type of temptation encountered

MOSES: Symbolic of the **OLD TESTAMENT LAW**. The law (and Moses) came before the **GRACE** of God through the death of Christ and therefore cannot offer **MERCY**.

CHRIST: The Son of God, the Redeemer and Saviour of all who look to him and believe.

DISCONTENT: Symbolises people who become disillusioned with their faith because it does not offer the immediate benefits expected.

SHAME: Symbolises people who are ashamed of the faith. They prefer to listen to current thinking and view religion as something for the ignorant. Their desire is to please people and think the impact of religion on believers is a 'shame'.

The VALLEY of the SHADOW of DEATH: Another symbol of the narrow and, at times, dark and dangerous road that leads to **HEAVEN**. The name reminds us of the well-known **Psalm 23** which contains the lines 'Even though I walk through the valley of the shadow of death, I will fear no evil, for you are with me' (v.4).

LIGHT/DAY and NIGHT: Light, in various forms, is used symbolically throughout the Bible to portray God and his Word. Here, Christian is able to see more clearly in the morning light, just as Christians see more clearly when they seek God, follow his Word and focus on Christ, the 'light' of the world. The contrast between day/night can also be compared with good/evil.

Did you know?

The Pilgrim's Progress has been translated into more than 200 languages to date.

Related Bible Verses and Texts

Psalm 23 'Even though I walk through the darkest valley, I will fear no evil, for you are with me' (v.4). (**The Valley of the Shadow of Death**)

Ephesians 6:18 'And pray in the Spirit on all occasions with all kinds of prayers and requests. With this in mind, be alert and always keep on praying for all the Lord's people.'

Acts 12:1-19 (*Peter's Miraculous Escape from Prison*) 'So Peter was kept in prison, but the church was earnestly praying to God for him.' (v.5) (**Prayer**)

Hebrews 11:1-40 (*By Faith*) This chapter gives examples of Biblical characters that lived by faith such as Enoch, Noah, Abraham, Isaac, Jacob, Joseph, Moses, Rahab and more. 'Now faith is confidence in what we hope for and assurance about what we do not see.' (v.1) (**Faithful/Faith**)

Romans 5:12-14 'Therefore, just as sin entered the world through one man, and death through sin, and in this way death came to all people, because all sinned.' (v.12) (See also **Genesis 3:1-24** *The Fall of Man*) (**Sin**)

Colossians 3:9 'Lie not one to another, seeing that ye have put off the old man with his deeds' (AV) (**Adam-the-First/Sin**)

Titus 3:4, 5 'But when the kindness and love of God our Saviour appeared, he saved us, not because of righteous things we had done, but because of his mercy.' (**Mercy**)

Ephesians 4:1-16 (*Unity in the Body of Christ*) 'From him the whole body, joined and held together by every supporting ligament, grows and builds itself up in love, as each part does its work.' (v.16) See also **Ecclesiastes 4:9** and **Acts 2: 42-47** (*The Fellowship of the Believers*) (**Christian Fellowship**)

1 John 1:5-10 (*Walking in the Light*) 'God is light; in him there is no darkness at all' (v.5); 'But if we walk in the light, as he is in the light, we have fellowship with one another, and the blood of Jesus, his Son, purifies us from all sin.' (v.7) (**Light/Darkness**)

Christian Concepts

FAITH, HOPE and LOVE: Known as the three Christian/theological virtues. See **1 Corinthians 13:13** 'And now these three remain: faith, hope and love. But the greatest of these is love'.

OLD TESTAMENT LAW: A guide given by God for his people to live by (see **Exodus 20:1-21**).

GRACE/MERCY: Words which describe the forgiveness and compassion shown by God in sending Christ as Saviour. Christ alone, through his death on the cross, has the power to save – the law is powerless to offer mercy/save.

PRAYER: Communion with God. Christians can pray anywhere and at any time. The Bible encourages Christians to 'pray continually' (see **1 Thessalonians 5:17**).

CHRISTIAN FELLOWSHIP: The Bible teaches the importance of Christian fellowship for encouraging and supporting one another. The word 'church' in Christian terms actually means the people, not the building.

Symbolism: Bunyan's 'Real-Life' Inspiration

FAITHFUL

Possibly inspired by Bunyan's friend William Dell, Rector of Yeldon. Dell was senior to Bunyan and an Anglican. Dell was ejected from his living as Rector in 1662. Whilst Bunyan significantly disagreed with the state church in matters of faith (hence his imprisonment) he chose his friends according to their faith not their denomination. Bunyan actually preached at Dell's church on Christmas Day 1659. This may be the reason why Faithful does not stop at the Palace Beautiful.

The VALLEY of the SHADOW of DEATH

The village of Millbrook lies west of Ampthill in a tree-lined gorge, part of the Greensand Ridge on the northern edge of the Chiltern Hills. Bunyan would have travelled through this gorge on journeys south from Bedford. In the dark this gorge would likely have appeared dark and gloomy and could be the inspiration for the Valley of the Shadow of Death.

Bunyan is likely to be remembering here the metrical version of **Psalm 23** by Thomas Sternhold and John Hopkin included in *The Whole Book of Psalms: Collected into English Meeter*. First published in 1549, this was a popular book in the 17th century.

The Story Explained...
2.6: Vanity Fair

Summary

CHRISTIAN and FAITHFUL continue on the journey together. They encounter TALKATIVE, son of SAYWELL, a character who can talk a lot about the Christian faith but whose life does not match what he talks about – he is 'all talk and no action'. The pilgrims talk together about the impact of faith on the life of a Christian. Trusting Christ will lead to a life of wanting to please God – in our actions as well as our words. Talkative does not like being challenged and walks off.

Christian and Faithful then meet their old friend EVANGELIST. He encourages them to stay on the right path, whatever the difficulties. He tells them that they will reach a town where they will not be liked and where one of them will die for the faith.

The town they reach is called VANITY FAIR. The people of this town are focused on things of the world ('vanities') and perceive the pilgrims as a threat. Christian and Faithful are taken prisoner and the townspeople encouraged to mock and insult them. Christian and Faithful do not retaliate but take their imprisonment graciously, which impresses a few of the townsfolk. This causes a skirmish which results in Christian and Faithful being taken off for trial. One of the onlookers is moved by the patience of the pilgrims. His name is HOPEFUL and he later becomes a believer due to their witness and joins Christian on his journey.

The pilgrims are taken to trial before a judge and a jury. The judge is called LORD HATEGOOD. A number of witnesses are called including ENVY, SUPERSTITION and PICKTHANK. Faithful defends the faith, condemning BEELZEBUB and all his followers. As a result, the judge and the jury vote unanimously that Faithful is guilty of treason and should be put to death.

Key Characters and Symbolism

CHRISTIAN and FAITHFUL: Enter the town prepared for difficulties. They remain steadfast under persecution, even though it means imprisonment and, for Faithful, death. The Bible teaches that we must be FAITHFUL 'even to the point of death' (**Revelation 2:10**)

TALKATIVE: Lives up to his name. Talks a lot about religion but does not follow through with his actions or way of life. When challenged, he walks off. This character is symbolic of those that allow their religion to go no deeper than their talk. The importance of action as well as words is emphasised by Bunyan in his allegory. This is the outward testimony of true spiritual transformation and requires a work of grace in the heart as well as the head/mind. In *The Pilgrim's Progress* Bunyan particularly emphasises the place of the HEART in the work of grace and the life of the Christian.

SAYWELL: His name describes his character, much like his son Talkative.

EVANGELIST: Spiritual guide. In this scene he shows his ability for prophecy (seeing the future) named in the Bible as one of the gifts of the Holy Spirit.

HOPEFUL: Becomes Christian's new companion after Faithful is martyred. Named after another of the three theological virtues – hope.

LORD HATEGOOD: As his name describes, he hates all that is good. His prince is Captain Beelzebub.

ENVY: As his name describes.

SUPERSTITION: As his name describes, symbolic of the type of beliefs held in Vanity Fair.

PICKTHANK: A man who is nice to people in authority and anyone who can do him a favour in return.

BEELZEBUB: Another name for the devil, the enemy of God and prince of Vanity Fair.

VANITY FAIR: Symbolic of all the 'vanities' (meaningless things) that the world is consumed by. The Bible teaches that Christians are merely passing through this world and should have their sight on spiritual things that are heavenly (ETERNAL), rather than on worldly things that are temporary and meaningless (TEMPORAL).

Related Bible Verses and Texts

James 1:22-27 'Do not merely listen to the word, and so deceive yourselves. Do what it says. Anyone who listens to the word but does not do what it says is like someone who looks at his face in a mirror and, after looking at himself, goes away and immediately forgets what he looks like.' (v.22-24)
James 2:26 'As the body without the spirit is dead, so faith without deeds is dead.' (**Talkative**)

Psalm 119:34 'Give me understanding, so that I may keep your law and obey it with all my heart.' (**Heart**)

Ephesians 4:11 'So Christ himself gave the apostles, the prophets, the evangelists, and the pastors and teachers.' (**Evangelist/Prophecy**)

Ecclesiastes 1:2 and **Ecclesiastes 12:8** 'Vanity of vanities, saith the Preacher, vanity of vanities; all is vanity.' (AV)

Hebrews 11:16 'Instead, they were longing for a better country – a heavenly one. Therefore God is not ashamed to be called their God, for he has prepared a city for them.' (**Vanity Fair/Temporal vs Eternal**)

Proverbs 23:23 'Buy the truth and do not sell it; wisdom, instruction and insight as well.' (**Christian/Faithful**)

Christian Concepts

The HEART: The Bible (in both the Old and New Testament) explicitly connects the heart with faith. See **Matthew 6:21** 'For where your treasure is, there your heart will be also'; **Psalm 111:1** 'I will praise the Lord with my whole heart' (AV); **Ecclesiastes 8:5** 'and the wise heart will know the proper time and procedure'; **John 14:1** 'Do not let your hearts be troubled. You believe in God; believe also in me'; **Ephesians 6:5** ' '…and with sincerity of heart, just as you would obey Christ'; and **Acts 8:21** '…because your heart is not right before God'.

FAITH: One of the three theological virtues as defined by St. Paul. Christians are called to be **FAITHFUL** in all things, just as God is faithful. See **Deuteronomy 32:4** 'He is the Rock, his works are perfect, and all his ways are just. A faithful God who does no wrong, upright and just is he'; and **1 Corinthians 4:2** 'Now it is required that those who have been given a trust must prove faithful.'

TEMPORAL vs ETERNAL: The temporal refers to earthly life and the eternal to the heavenly one. The Bible teaches that we should store up treasures in heaven, not on earth (see **Matthew 6:19,20**).

Symbolism: Bunyan's 'Real-Life' Inspiration

TALKATIVE

No doubt Talkative was inspired by the many people Bunyan would have encountered who spoke much of religion but did not practice it in their daily lives, for example: some academics (he was not anti-intellectual, just against those that only had an intellectual awareness of the truth), false professors or ministers (such as Rev. Christopher Hall, the vicar of Elstow who, evidence suggests, did not practice what he preached) and those in office who promoted the state religion but did not uphold it.

LORD HATEGOOD

Sir John Kelynge of Southill, a barrister, was one of five judges on the bench which judged John Bunyan when he was first sent to prison. Bunyan was inspired by Sir John Kelynge when creating the character Lord Hategood of Vanity Fair.

VANITY FAIR

Bunyan was likely to be inspired by the fair held every September at Stourbridge near Cambridge. This was one of the greatest of English fairs and very large. Tents were arranged in rows like streets and goods from around England as well as from abroad would have been on sale. There would also have been jugglers, actors, puppet-shows and other entertainment. The fair would also have had its own court for offenders. Rev. John Brown describes the fair in some detail in his biography of Bunyan (first edition 1885/revised edition 1928).

The Story Explained...
2.7: Faith, Hope and Love

Summary

FAITHFUL is tried and condemned to death by burning. But unknown to the jeering crowd, Faithful is taken up to heaven in a horse-drawn chariot. CHRISTIAN on the other hand, has been thrown into prison. But God is in control and Christian is able to escape and continue on his way with a new companion – HOPEFUL. Hopeful had been impressed by the WITNESS of both Faithful and Christian and as a result had become 'Christian'.

They travel together, meeting various characters along the way – all false pilgrims. Eventually they reach the PLAIN of EASE, a small plain that is easy to cross. At the end of it they pause to look at the silver mines at the bottom of a small hill called LUCRE. Here they meet DEMAS, son of JUDAS THE TRAITOR, who tries to persuade them to leave the path and take a look at the mine. Christian realises the trick and walks away quickly with Hopeful.

Next they come to a beautiful resting place where they stay a few days for important rest, relaxation and refreshment. They drink water from the RIVER of the WATER of LIFE and are able to continue on their way feeling stronger and fitter for the journey. The path, though, soon becomes difficult and the pilgrims spot BY-PATH MEADOW – a much smoother path running close by which tempts them. Hopeful is cautious but Christian persuades him. They meet a man walking the same way who tells them he is on his way to the heavenly city. His name is VAIN-CONFIDENCE. Unfortunately, he passes this unfounded confidence on to the pilgrims and they continue on their way, oblivious that they are walking towards real danger. Night comes and with it a thunder storm forcing the pilgrims to take shelter under a tree.

In the morning the pilgrims are woken by GIANT DESPAIR who accuses them of trespass – they are in the grounds of DOUBTING CASTLE. The Giant throws them into his dark, smelly dungeon and locks them up. The pilgrims feel dreadful as they realise they are in grave danger. But Christian is also feeling guilty for leading them both astray, even though Hopeful has assured Christian that he FORGIVES him. What will happen to them?

Key Characters and Symbolism

FAITHFUL: Lives up to his name and calling, he is 'Faithful' even unto death. But he is rewarded by being taken up to heaven in a chariot, a reference to the biblical character Elijah who was taken up to heaven in a chariot of fire (see 2 Kings 2:11).

CHRISTIAN: Remains steadfast throughout the trial and imprisonment. He is maturing as a Christian and understands that God is SOVEREIGN – nothing happens that is outside of God's control/GOD'S PROVIDENCE. As Christian experiences more of life – both good and bad – he is able to see God's hand in everything and this helps him to trust God in good times as well as bad. But as we see towards the end of the chapter, a mature faith does not mean one free of mistakes.

HOPEFUL: Christian's new companion. Like Faithful, Hopeful's character is reflected in his name. He has been converted through the witness of Faithful and Christian at Vanity Fair but, in contrast to Christian, his experience was more straightforward – the Wicket-gate and the cross were experienced together. In the original version Bunyan's describes it as 'believing and coming was all one'.

DEMAS, son of JUDAS: A reference to a character in the Bible who the apostle Paul refers to in 2 Timothy 4:10. Demas loved the world and deserted Paul. Judas is a reference to the biblical Judas who betrayed Christ for 30 pieces of silver.

VAIN-CONFIDENCE: Lives up to his name. His confidence has no foundation unlike the true pilgrim whose foundation is Christ.

GIANT DESPAIR: A symbol of the 'giant despair' pilgrims can feel when they are overcome with doubt.

PLAIN of EASE: A part of the journey that offers ease and contentment. The plain is small and narrow, symbolic of the small amount of ease that Christians should expect in this life.

LUCRE: Lucre (meaning money) is mentioned in 1 Samuel 8:3 (Samuel's sons 'turned aside after lucre') and in Timothy, Titus and Peter in the NT ('filthy lucre').

RIVER of the WATER of LIFE: Symbolises another of the rest places and comforts that God provides for his pilgrims along the way. Here Bunyan is referring to the 'river of God' (Psalm 65:9) and 'a pure river of water of life, clear as crystal' (Revelation 22:1) (AV)

BY-PATH MEADOW: Symbolic of the more tempting, easier paths through life.

DOUBTING CASTLE: Symbolic of how dark and terrible times of DOUBT can be to a Christian.

Did you know?

Bunyan only made significant additions to the second and third editions of *The Pilgrim's Progress*.

Related Bible Verses and Texts

Revelation 2:10 'Do not be afraid of what you are about to suffer. I tell you, the devil will put some of you in prison to test you, and you will suffer persecution for ten days. Be faithful, even to the point of death, and I will give you life as your victor's crown.' (**Faithful**)

1 Corinthians 13:13 'And now these three remain: faith, hope and love. But the greatest of these is love.'
Colossians 1:27 '…which is Christ in you, the hope of glory.'
1 Peter 3:15 'But in your hearts revere Christ as Lord. Always be prepared to give an answer to everyone who asks you to give the reason for the hope that you have.' (**Hopeful**)

Mark 16:15 'He said to them, 'Go into all the world and preach the gospel to all creation.'

Acts 22:15 'You will be his witness to all people of what you have seen and heard.' (**Witness**)

Psalm 23:2 'He makes me lie down in green pastures, he leads me beside quiet waters, he restores my soul.' (**Plain of Ease**)

Ezekiel 47 (*The River from the Temple*) 'Fruit trees of all kinds will grow on both banks of the river. Their leaves will not wither, nor will their fruit fail. Every month they will bear fruit, because the water from the sanctuary flows to them. Their fruit will serve for food and their leaves for healing.' (v.12) (**River of the Water of Life**)

Matthew 14:22-33 (*Jesus Walks on the Water*) 'Immediately Jesus reached out his hand and caught him.' 'You of little faith,' he said, 'why did you doubt?' (v.31) (**Giant Despair/Doubting Castle**)

1 Timothy 6:10 'For the love of money is a root of all kinds of evil. Some people, eager for money, have wandered from the faith and pierced themselves with many griefs.' (**Demas/Judas/Lucre**)

Christian Concepts

HOPE: Another of the three theological virtues, symbolised here by the character Hopeful. The biblical 'hope' refers to the hope Christians have through the death of Christ on the cross which offers forgiveness of sins and the promise of eternal life for all who believe (see **1 Thessalonians 4:13-18**, *The Coming of the Lord*).

WITNESS/EVANGELISM: The Bible teaches that believers have a responsibility to live in a way that honours God and to tell the world about the good news of Christ.

FORGIVENESS: A key theme throughout the Bible, particularly in the gospel message – we are offered forgiveness of sins and the promise of eternal life if we look to Christ and believe. We are also commanded to forgive one another, just as Christ forgives us (see **Ephesians 4:32**). In this chapter Christian, the more mature pilgrim, has led Hopeful away from the right path and into danger. Hopeful sees his distress and forgives him saying 'Be comforted my Brother, for I forgive thee; and believe too, that this shall be for our good.' (Original version). The last part of this sentence particularly demonstrates Hopeful's strength of faith and wisdom, for believers are promised that God will make everything work for good – even difficult times and mistakes. (**Romans 8:28** 'And we know that in all things God works for the good of those who love him, who have been called according to his purpose.')

GOD'S SOVEREIGNTY/PROVIDENCE: This means God-given. The Bible teaches that God is in control of everything – he is sovereign. Bunyan uses the phrase 'As God would have it' a number of times in the original version to convey this belief.

FAITH and DOUBT: The Bible acknowledges that believers will have times of doubt but gives frequent encouragement to have faith in God (see **Mark 11:22-24**). Bunyan himself had times of intense doubt which he describes in his spiritual autobiography *Grace Abounding*. However, times of doubt can make faith stronger, as Christian and Hopeful found from their experience in Doubting Castle.

FAITH, HOPE and LOVE: The three theological virtues, represented in *The Pilgrim's Progress* by the characters Faithful and Hopeful and by the gospel message – God showing his love in sending his Son to die on the cross (see **John 3:16**).

Symbolism: Bunyan's 'Real-Life' Inspiration

FAITHFUL'S DEATH
Portraying Faithful's death in this way Bunyan would have had in mind some of the illustrations from Foxe's *Acts and Monuments* (popularly known as Foxe's *Book of Martyrs*). This is one of the two books that we know Bunyan had with him in prison.

GIANT DESPAIR
Bunyan would have been inspired by the giants of popular folk tales and romances for the characters of Giant Despair and his wife Diffidence.

The Story Explained...
2.8: Faith and Doubt

Summary

GIANT DESPAIR and his wife DIFFIDENCE discuss what to do with the pilgrims that they have locked away in their dungeon in DOUBTING CASTLE. Diffidence has no sympathy with pilgrims on their way to heaven and wants them dead. When her husband fails to kill them she suggests Giant Despair gives them tools which they can use to kill themselves – she wants him to persuade them that suicide is their best option out of such despair. CHRISTIAN is feeling much weaker than HOPEFUL and suggests they do as they are told. At least it would end their despair. But Hopeful disagrees, reminding him that suicide is forbidden by God. Living up to his name, he speaks of all those that have previously escaped from the Castle and reminds Christian of all the dangers they have already come through.

Diffidence, impatient to get rid of the pilgrims, tells Giant Despair to show them the bones of pilgrims who did not make it. The pilgrims look in horror at the sight of all the bones and have to endure another beating before being thrown back into the dungeon. But they still do not give up. Instead, they spent the night in prayer. In the morning, Christian suddenly remembers the KEY OF PROMISE given to him at the cross. The Key opens the door of the dungeon and they are able to escape. They cross the meadow and find their way back on to the right path, but before continuing on their journey they stop to write a sign warning other pilgrims not to stray into BY-PATH MEADOW – as more mature pilgrims their minds are on the welfare of future pilgrims as well as themselves.

Christian and Hopeful continue on their way, singing and praising God as they travel.

Key Characters and Symbolism

CHRISTIAN and HOPEFUL: Symbolic of the persevering Christian, who, even in the face of wrong decisions and difficult times, continues to stand firm in faith, trusting God in everything. But, as for Christian here, fellow pilgrims (like Hopeful) provide much needed support and encouragement in moments of weakness, despair and doubt.

GIANT DESPAIR: Symbolic of the despair that can overwhelm Christians at times, especially during times of difficulty and challenge (such as illness, bereavement, financial difficulties etc).

DIFFIDENCE: Symbolic of distrust, doubt and low self-esteem resulting in a jealousy and hatred of anything or anyone that appears confident and assured – as the pilgrims appeared with regard to their faith and love of God. Here, Diffidence is the driving force behind the torture of the pilgrims and the desire to see them dead.

DOUBTING CASTLE: Symbolic of the potentially huge impact that DOUBT can have on a true pilgrim. Not every Christian will struggle with doubt. Christian was the one to lead Hopeful out of the way and it was Christian who contemplated suicide. Hopeful remained steadfast and once again lives up to his name – he remains 'Hopeful' in the face of death and despair.

BY-PATH MEADOW: Symbolic of the temptations pilgrims face along the way. The Bible teaches that the road to heaven is narrow and that Christians should expect suffering. When easier ways are in sight they can be hard to resist but often are not the right way and bring trouble.

KEY of PROMISE: Christian was given this at the cross. It symbolises the many passages of Scripture that remind believers of the promises God has given us through his Word. When Christian realised he had this Key, he was able to bring to mind examples of these verses/texts which gave him the strength to unlock the (symbolic) dungeon of despair and doubt and continue on the journey with renewed faith.

I really enjoyed studying *The Pilgrim's Progress*… What I enjoyed the most watching plus reading about *The Pilgrim's Progress*. I also liked doing the drama. What I liked the least is nothing I didn't like. When we went to the museum I really enjoyed it. It was interesting seeing so many things about John Bunyan and getting a famous writer's autograph (Peter Morden). I will remember watching *The Pilgrim's Progress*. I will remember: the fight against Apollyon, The Dark River, Doubting Castle, Losing the Burden.

Related Bible Verses and Texts

Philippians 1:4-5 'In all my prayers for all of you, I always pray with joy because of your partnership in the gospel from the first day until now, being confident of this, that he who began a good work in you will carry it on to completion until the day of Christ Jesus.'

Ecclesiastes 4:9-10 'Two are better than one, because they have a good return for their labour. If either of them falls down, one can help the other up. But pity anyone who falls and has no-one to help them up.' (**Christian/Hopeful**)

2 Corinthians 1:8-11 'We were under great pressure, far beyond our ability to endure, so that we despaired of life itself. Indeed, we felt we had received the sentence of death. But this happened that we might not rely on ourselves but on God, who raises the dead.' (v. 8/9)

2 Corinthians 4:8-9 ' We are hard pressed on every side, but not crushed; perplexed, but not in despair; persecuted, but not abandoned; struck down, but not destroyed.' (**Giant Despair/Diffidence**)

John 20:24-31 'Then he said to Thomas, 'Put your finger here; see my hands. Reach out your hand and put it into my side. Stop doubting and believe.' (v. 27) 'But these are written that you may believe that Jesus is the Messiah, the Son of God, and that by believing you may have life in his name.' (v.31) (**Doubt/Doubting Castle**)

Mark 10:23-31 'But Jesus said again, 'Children, how hard it is to enter the kingdom of God! It is easier for a camel to go through the eye of a needle than for someone who is rich to enter the kingdom of God.' (v.24/25) (**By-Path Meadow**)

Acts 12 (*Peter's Miraculous Escape from Prison*) 'Now I know without a doubt that the Lord has sent his angel and rescued me from Herod's clutches and from everything the Jewish people were hoping would happen.' (v.11)

Philippians 4:13 'I can do all this through him who gives me strength.' (**Key of Promise**)

Christian Concepts

DOUBT: A feeling of uncertainty with regard to faith; to mistrust or call into question either God's love or the very existence of God. Christians can experience both kinds of doubt.

OBEDIENCE: Christians are called to obey (to follow), God and God's word.

HOPE: One of the three theological virtues. Christians are promised hope for this life and for the next (see **2 Thessalonians 2:16**).

PATIENCE: The Bible encourages Christians to be patient – with God (especially for answers to prayer) and with others (see **Romans 12:12**, **1 Thessalonians 5:14**).

PRAYER: The Bible teaches that we can pray directly to God. Jesus taught the disciples how to pray and this prayer is called the Lord's Prayer (see **Luke 11:2-4**). Prayers should include praise, thanksgiving, repentance and requests. The Bible teaches that we should pray continually (see **1 Thessalonians 5:17**) and not give up (see **Luke 18:1-8**).

Symbolism: Bunyan's 'Real-Life' Inspiration

DOUBTING CASTLE	Bunyan himself struggled for a number of years with huge doubts, not just about his own salvation but about the very existence of God. He speaks of this latter type of doubt in *Grace Abounding* as being 'the worst, and the worst to bear'.
GIANT DESPAIR	Inspired by the giants of folk-tales and the popular romances of the time.
HOPEFUL	Hopeful's speech encouraging Christian not to give up is reminiscent, in parts, of the famous words of Bishop Latimer to Bishop Ridley as they were being burned at the stake in Oxford. This is recorded in Foxe's *Book of Martyrs*, one of two books that Bunyan had in prison with him (the other being the Bible).

The Story Explained...
2.9: Knowledge and Experience

Summary

CHRISTIAN and HOPEFUL arrive at the DELECTABLE MOUNTAINS, part of IMMANUEL'S LAND. Here they meet the shepherds and spend some time with them. Their names are: SINCERE, WATCHFUL, KNOWLEDGE and EXPERIENCE. As their names suggest they are full of WISDOM and knowledge and are able to teach the pilgrims many things. The shepherds also show the pilgrims some important sights, all of which help them to grow spiritually: the HILL of ERROR that some pilgrims had fallen from; a peak called CAUTION, from where they could see pilgrims captured by Giant Despair, unable to find their way out of the darkness; the BY-WAY to HELL for those who chose worldly pleasures above eternal; the hill called CLEAR with a telescope that enabled them to catch a glimpse of the gates to the Celestial City. After giving them direction to the Celestial City and warning them to be aware of the Flatterer and the Enchanted Ground, the shepherds wish them well and send them on their way.

Christian tells Hopeful the tale of LITTLE-FAITH, from the TOWN OF SINCERE. Little-Faith was set upon by three villains, MISTRUST, GUILT and FAINT-HEART. Little-Faith fought back and managed to keep hold of his jewels and his scroll, but because of his 'little faith' was badly injured (physically and spiritually) and never fully recovered.

Christian and Hopeful continue on their journey until they come to a fork in the road. A stranger gives them the wrong directions and they find themselves trapped by the FLATTERER. An ANGEL appeared to rescue them, but also gives them a severe telling off for not heeding the advice of the shepherds. Further along the road they meet ATHEIST who laughs when they tell him they are on their way to heaven. But the pilgrims have learnt their lesson with the Flatterer and do not waste time listening to Atheist. They arrive at the ENCHANTED GROUND but with the words of the shepherds and the angel ringing in their ears they refuse to succumb to the sleep-inducing air by talking to each other about their Christian journey and particularly, Hopeful's conversion.

Key Characters and Symbolism

KNOWLEDGE, SINCERE, WATCHFUL, EXPERIENCE: Four shepherds living on the Delectable Mountains. Their names are symbolic of their characters and all of them are keen to help pilgrims grow in grace by passing onto them their spiritual 'knowledge' and 'experience'.

LITTLE FAITH: This character is symbolic of true pilgrims who have assurance of salvation but who are only capable of 'little faith'. Bunyan wanted to reassure pilgrims that not every pilgrim will have great faith or do great things for God. The important thing is the genuineness of faith, whether great or 'little', and the need to hold on to it, as Little Faith did.

MISTRUST: Like the name, someone who doesn't trust.

GUILT: Symbolic of the name. Christians often find it difficult to forgive themselves even though they accept that God has forgiven them. Continuing guilt can be a block to making progress in the Christian life.

FAINT-HEART: As the name suggests a character with a weak heart/character.

FLATTERER: This character represents false ministers, who mislead and confuse pilgrims whilst initially appearing to help them – hence the net that Christian and Hopeful find themselves trapped in.

ANGEL: One of God's messengers/helpers, sent to rescue the pilgrims. The Bible promises that God will send angels to watch over pilgrims as they journey through life.

ATHEIST: Symbolises people who refuse to believe in the existence of God.

DELECTABLE MOUNTAINS: Part of Immanuel's Land – the land belonging to the Prince (Christ). Immanuel is a biblical name for Christ (see Isaiah 7:14).

BY-WAY to HELL: A warning that the path is still not necessarily safe for pilgrims.

HILL of ERROR, CAUTION: Symbolic of the dangers of the Christian journey which continue, even as pilgrims mature in faith.

CLEAR: Symbolic of the clarity of faith a Christian experiences the closer he/she gets to Christ.

TOWN of SINCERE: Where Little-Faith came from, an indication that his faith is real.

ENCHANTED GROUND: A beautiful but dangerous place that tempts pilgrims to sleep.

Related Bible Verses and Texts

Isaiah 7:14 'Therefore the Lord himself will give you a sign: The virgin will conceive and give birth to a son, and will call him Immanuel.' (**Immanuel's Land**)

John 10 'I am the good shepherd. The good shepherd lays down his life for the sheep.' (v.11)
Colossians 1:9-10 'For this reason, since the day we heard about you, we have not stopped praying for you. We continually ask God to fill you with the knowledge of his will through all the wisdom and understanding that the Spirit gives, so that you may live a life worthy of the Lord and please him in every way: bearing fruit in every good work, growing in the knowledge of God.'
(**The Shepherds – Knowledge, Experience, Sincere, Watchful**)

Hosea 14:9 'Who is wise? Let them realize these things. Who is discerning? Let them understand. The ways of the Lord are right; the righteous walk in them, but the rebellious stumble in them.'
(**By-Way to Hell/Wisdom**)

Proverbs 4 'The beginning of wisdom is this; get wisdom. Though it cost all you have, get understanding.' (v.7)
Proverbs 16:16 'How much better to get wisdom than gold, to get insight rather than silver!'
(**Wisdom**)

1 Corinthians 13:12 'For now we see only a reflection in a mirror; then we shall see face to face. Now I know in part; then I shall know fully, even as I am fully known.' (**Clear**)

Romans 6:14 'For sin shall no longer be your master, because you are not under the law, but under grace.' (**Guilt**)

2 Timothy 1:14 'Guard the good deposit that was entrusted to you – guard it with the help of the Holy Spirit who lives in us.' (**Little-Faith**)

Proverbs 29:5 'Those who flatter their neighbours are spreading nets for their feet.'
Romans 16:18 'For such people are not serving our Lord Christ, but their own appetites. By smooth talk and flattery they deceive the minds of naïve people.' (**Flatterer**)

Psalm 34:7 'The angel of the Lord encamps around those who fear him, and he delivers them.' (**Angel**)

Psalm 14:1, 53:1 'The fool says in his heart, 'There is no God'.'
2 Corinthians 5:7 'We live by faith, not by sight.' (see also **2 Corinthians 4:4**) (**Atheist**)

Christian Concepts

WISDOM: Knowledge and sound judgement/understanding in spiritual matters, something that is often gained through experience, though not always (see **Job 32:7-9** 'I thought, 'Age should speak; advanced years should teach wisdom.' But it is the spirit in a person, the breath of the Almighty, that gives them understanding. It is not only the old who are wise, nor only the aged who understand what is right.') The Bible speaks much of the need for wisdom and understanding – see particularly the book of **Proverbs** in the Old Testament.

Symbolism: Bunyan's 'Real-Life' Inspiration

DELECTABLE MOUNTAINS	Inspired by the Chiltern Hills (see notes to story Chapter 2.4: **Apollyon**)
FLATTERER	Very possibly inspired by the many false 'professors' (ministers) that Bunyan would have come across during his lifetime.

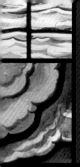

The Story Explained...
2.10: The Celestial City

Summary

CHRISTIAN and HOPEFUL arrive at a country called BEULAH, on the borders of heaven. It is a beautiful country where the pilgrims can wander free of the dangers that they had previously encountered along the way. They meet a GARDENER who assures them that the land is owned and cared for by the King, for the benefit of pilgrims. The country is so wonderful and relaxing that it makes the pilgrims long even more for their arrival at the CELESTIAL CITY.

They meet TWO ANGELS who tell them there are two challenges left before they will arrive at the Celestial City. The first is the RIVER of DEATH, the second a STEEP HILL that leads directly up to the Celestial City. When they reach the heavenly gates they are met by a welcome party and much music. At the top of the gates they see three men looking down at them – ENOCH, MOSES and ELIJAH – great men of the Old Testament. Christian and Hopeful hand over their SCROLLS to the men. The gates of heaven are opened and they are welcomed inside. The pilgrims have arrived safely at their long-desired destination – the Celestial City.

NOTE: The original version of *The Pilgrim's Progress* ends with the character IGNORANCE trying to get into heaven. But he has no Scroll and is judged not to be a true pilgrim. He is bound hand and foot by angels and taken to HELL.

Key Characters and Symbolism

GARDENER: Garden imagery is used frequently in the Bible, symbolic of creation, life, beauty, peace, tranquillity (two key examples: Garden of Eden, Garden of Gethsemane). In John 20:15 the risen Christ appears to Mary in the garden where he had been buried, and she mistakes him for the gardener.

TWO ANGELS: Angels are God's aids or messengers who are sent by God at particular times to help his people. Angels are mentioned much in connection with death and heaven in the final book of the Bible, the book of Revelation.

ENOCH, MOSES, ELIJAH: Three significant men of the Old Testament. Moses was given the law by God in the Old Testament, Enoch and Elijah were the only two men in the Bible to enter heaven without passing through the River of Death.

IGNORANCE: The character Ignorance is symbolic of people who think they have a secure faith but who are actually ignorant of the real gospel and the meaning of grace. Bunyan would have been thinking of those caught up in the state religion at the time and the presentation of Christian belief based on works/the law.

BEULAH: The name means 'married' and is the name the prophet Isaiah says will be given to the land of Israel.

CELESTIAL CITY/HEAVEN: The destination Christian set out for at the start of his pilgrimage – the promised destination of all true Christians.

RIVER of DEATH: Symbolic of death itself. Death came to all humanity because of the Fall – the sin of Adam and Eve in the Garden of Eden when they disobeyed God and ate of the Tree of the Knowledge of Good and Evil. For Christians, the River of Death is described as 'deeper or shallower' according to their strength of faith.

STEEP HILL: Leads to the Celestial City, which is set on a steep hill. This is the final hurdle after the River of Death but one that is easy for believers because they leave their 'mortal garments' at the River of Death and have angels to lead them up.

SCROLLS: Certificates given to believers at the cross. The Scroll represents salvation, so only pilgrims who have this Scroll when they arrive at the Celestial City are allowed in. At the end of *The Pilgrim's Progress* we are told that Ignorance does not have such a Scroll – he has arrived under false pretences – and he is not allowed in.

HELL: The opposite to heaven, an eternity without God. The Bibles teaches that this is where all who have not made a true confession of faith in Jesus Christ in this life will spend eternity. In the Bible hell is often symbolised by fire.

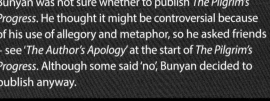

Did you know?

Bunyan was not sure whether to publish *The Pilgrim's Progress*. He thought it might be controversial because of his use of allegory and metaphor, so he asked friends – see '*The Author's Apology*' at the start of *The Pilgrim's Progress*. Although some said 'no', Bunyan decided to publish anyway.

Related Bible Verses and Texts

John 20:15 'Thinking he was the gardener, she said, 'Sir, if you have carried him away, tell me where you have put him, and I will get him.' (**Gardener**)

Hebrews 1:14 'Are not all angels ministering spirits sent to serve those who will inherit salvation?' (**Angels**)

Hebrews 11: 5 'By faith Enoch was taken from this life, so that he did not experience death; He could not be found, because God had taken him away.' (**Enoch**) also 2 Kings 2: 11 (**Elijah**)

Exodus 19: 9 'The Lord said to Moses, 'I am going to come to you in a dense cloud. So that people will hear me speaking with you and will always put their trust in you.' (**Moses**)

Proverbs 28:26 'Those who trust in themselves are fools, but those who walk in wisdom are kept safe.' (**Ignorance**)

Isaiah 62:4 '...But you will be called Hephzibah, and your land Beulah, for the Lord will take delight in you, and your land will be married.' (**Beulah**)

Hebrews 12:22 'But you have come to Mount Zion, to the city of the living God, the heavenly Jerusalem.' (**Celestial City/Heaven**)

Romans 5:12 'Therefore, just as sin entered the world through one man, and death through sin, and in this way death came to all people, because all sinned…'
Psalm 18:4, 5 'The cords of death entangled me; the torrents of destruction overwhelmed me. The cords of the grave coiled around me; the snares of death confronted me.' (**River of Death**)

Acts 4:12 'Salvation is found in no-one else, for there is no other name under heaven given to men under which we must be saved.' (**Scrolls/Salvation**)

Mark 9:47, 48 'It is better for you to enter the kingdom of God with one eye than to have two eyes and be thrown into hell, where the worms that eat them do not die, and the fire is not quenched.' (**Hell**)

Christian Concepts

DEATH: The Bible teaches that physical death came to humanity as a result of the Fall, when Adam and Eve disobeyed God by taking the fruit from the Tree of the Knowledge of Good and Evil (see **Genesis 3**).

SALVATION: The saving of the soul from the spiritual and eternal consequences of evil/wrongdoing/ sin. The Bible teaches that Jesus Christ is the Saviour who brings salvation to humanity.

HEAVEN: The place where God lives (**Psalm 14:2**) and an eternity with God. The Bible promises 'eternal life' to those who believe in Jesus Christ as the Son of God (**John 3:16**) (see also **Revelation 21**).

HELL: An eternity without God, often symbolized in the Bible by fire (see **Luke 16:19-31** *The Rich Man and Lazarus*).

ANGELS: Divine beings. There are good angels and fallen angels. The Bible teaches that God sends good angels to watch over us (see **Psalm 91:11**).

Symbolism: Bunyan's 'Real-Life' Inspiration

IGNORANCE

Bunyan would have been thinking particularly of those caught up in the state religion at that time and the presentation of a Christian belief based on works/the law. In the original version there is an extended conversation between Ignorance and Christian just before the pilgrims reach the country of Beulah. Ignorance does not like or agree with the beliefs Christian expounds and so tells Christian and Hopeful to carry on without him and he will follow at his own pace. The final paragraph sees Ignorance crossing the River of Death and trying to get into heaven. He fails. Angels are instructed to bind him and cast him into hell. Ending *The Pilgrim's Progress* with Ignorance being cast into hell reflects Bunyan's strong disagreement with the state religion and his passionate desire that people should know and understand biblical truth.

Did you know?

Since the first publication of *The Pilgrim's Progress* in 1678 it has never been out of print.

Chapter 3
Curriculum

CHRISTIAN VANQUISHES THE FIEND APOLLYON

A more unequal match can hardly be,
Christian must fight an Angel; but you see,
The valiant man by handling Sword and Shield,
Doth make him, tho' a Dragon, quit the field.

3.1: Suggested Scheme of Work

Week/Lesson 1

	KS1 (Y1/2)	**LKS2** (Y3/4)	**UKS2** (Y5/6)
Learning Objective	To appreciate the background to *The Pilgrim's Progress* – Who wrote it, why and when?	To appreciate the background to *The Pilgrim's Progress* – Who wrote it, why and when?	To appreciate the background to *The Pilgrim's Progress* – Who wrote it, why and when?
Content	Introduce the book and its author. Explain who John Bunyan was and why he went to prison. Why he wrote books, especially *The Pilgrim's Progress*. When Bunyan was in prison and when he wrote the book. Facts about *The Pilgrim's Progress*.	Introduce the book and its author. Explain who John Bunyan was and why he went to prison. Why he wrote books, especially *The Pilgrim's Progress*. When Bunyan was in prison and when he wrote the book. Facts about *The Pilgrim's Progress*.	Introduce the book and its author. Explain who John Bunyan was and why he went to prison. Why he wrote books, especially *The Pilgrim's Progress*. When Bunyan was in prison and when he wrote the book. Facts about *The Pilgrim's Progress*.
Key Words	John Bunyan The Stuarts Puritans/Roundheads Pilgrim Progress Royalists/Cavaliers Faith Allegory	John Bunyan Non-conformist Puritans/Roundheads Pilgrim Progress Royalists/Cavaliers Faith Conversion The Stuarts Allegory	John Bunyan Faith Puritans/Roundheads Conversion/Justification Royalists/Cavaliers Sanctification/Progress The Stuarts Non-conformist Evangelism Pilgrim Allegory
Key Christian Concepts	Pilgrimage Puritan When obedience to God comes before obedience to the State/Government/Others Allegory	Pilgrimage Puritan Non-conformism **Conversion** Allegory	Pilgrimage **Sanctification** Puritan Evangelism Non-conformism Allegory **Conversion/Justification**
Suggested Activities	Telling the story of John Bunyan's life – the main points (birth, marriage/family, conversion and imprisonment, pastorate of Bunyan Meeting, second imprisonment, writing, and death). Choose 5 facts about *The Pilgrim's Progress* to tell the class. Class to draw a picture of the book and write the facts underneath.	Telling the story of John Bunyan's life – the main points (birth, marriage/family, conversion and imprisonment, pastorate of Bunyan Meeting, second imprisonment, writing, and death). Timeline of Bunyan's life with national events – questions (knowledge and understanding). Choose 10 facts about *The Pilgrim's Progress* to share with the class. Class to write a paragraph or two about the book and its author.	Telling the story of John Bunyan's life – the main points (birth, marriage/family, conversion and imprisonment, pastorate of Bunyan Meeting, second imprisonment, writing, and death). Timeline of Bunyan's life with national events – questions (knowledge and understanding). Choose 10 facts about *The Pilgrim's Progress* to share with the class. Class to design a leaflet about the book and its author.
Plenary	What is an allegory? Think of an allegorical name to describe them and write it down (to use for introduction to next lesson). Give some examples first. Focus on positive names.	What is an allegory? Think of an allegorical name to describe them and write it down (to use for introduction to next lesson). Give some examples first. Discuss whether names are positive or negative.	What is an allegory? Think of an allegorical name to describe them and write it down. Ask for some examples from the class first. Discuss whether examples are positive or negative.
Suggested Enrichment Activities (home/school)	Find out more about: The English Civil War The Great Plague The Great Fire of London	Find out more about: The English Civil War The Great Plague The Great Fire of London The execution of Charles I	Finish leaflets Find out more about: The English Civil War The Great Plague The Great Fire of London The execution of Charles I Oliver Cromwell

Colour coding key

RED	Characters names from *The Pilgrim's Progress*
GREEN	Symbolic objects and places found in *The Pilgrim's Progress*
BLUE	Key Christian words/concepts
BOLD	Bible verses/references

Week/Lesson 2

	KS1 (Y1/2)	LKS2 (Y3/4)	UKS2 (Y5/6)
Learning Objective	To understand the importance of the **Bible** to the Christian faith; and the Christian concept of **sin**.	To understand the importance of the **Bible** to the Christian faith; and the Christian concept of **sin**.	To understand the importance of the **Bible** to the Christian faith; and the Christian concept of **sin**.
Content	Class to share allegorical names. Chapter 1 of *The Family Pilgrim's Progress*. Discuss names/symbolism as they arise. Focus on the '**Book**' and the '**Burden**' as key symbols. What do they represent? Why are they both important to the Christian faith?	Class to share allegorical names. Chapter 1 of *The Family Pilgrim's Progress*. Discuss names/symbolism as they arise. Focus on the '**Book**' and the '**Burden**' as key symbols. What do they represent? Why are they both important to the Christian faith?	Class to share allegorical names. Chapter 1 of *The Family Pilgrim's Progress*. Discuss names/symbolism as they arise. Focus on the '**Book**' and the '**Burden**' as key symbols. What do they represent? Why are they both important to the Christian faith?
Key Words	**Christian** · **Light** · **City of Destruction** · **Bible** · **Celestial City/ Heaven** · **Sin** · **Book** · **Jesus** · **Burden** · **Saviour**	**Christian** · **Light** · **City of Destruction** · **Bible** · **Celestial City/ Heaven** · **Sin** · **Book** · **Jesus** · **Burden** · **Saviour** · **Conversion**	**Christian** · **Bible** · **City of Destruction** · **Sin** · **Celestial City/ Heaven** · **Jesus** · **Book** · **Saviour** · **Burden** · **Conversion** · **Light** · **Justification** · **Sanctification** · **Glorification**
Key Christian Concepts	**The Bible/ Word of God** · **Jesus as Saviour** · **Sin** · **Christian** · **Heaven**	**The Bible/ Word of God** · **Christian** · **Sin** · **Conversion** · **Jesus as Saviour** · **Heaven**	**The Bible/ Word of God** · **Conversion** · **Sin** · **Heaven** · **Jesus as Saviour** · **Justification** · **Christian** · **Sanctification** · **Glorification**
Suggested Activities	Sharing allegorical names as a class. Discuss the difference between good/positive names and not so good/negative/bad names. Read Chapter 1. Display allegorical names from story on board (people, places and objects). Decide which are good and which not so good/bad. Divide class into two. One half to consider the '**Book**', the other the '**Burden**'. Draw a simple picture of either the book or the burden. In pairs, describe what it is and why it is important to the Christian faith.	Sharing allegorical names as a class. Discuss the difference between good/positive names and not so good/negative/bad names. Read Chapter 1. Display allegorical names from story on board (people, places and objects). Decide which are good and which not so good/bad. Draw a simple picture of the '**Book**' and the '**Burden**'. Describe what each is and why each is important to the Christian faith.	Sharing allegorical names as a class. Discuss the difference between good/positive names and not so good/negative/bad names. Read Chapter 1. Display allegorical names from story on board (people, places and objects). Decide which are good and which not so good/bad. Draw a simple picture of the '**Book**' and the '**Burden**'. Describe what each is and why each is important to the Christian faith, incorporating the key words and concepts.
Plenary	Children feedback their drawings and ideas to the whole class. Teacher writes a sentence to describe the '**Book**' and the '**Burden**' on the board for the class to copy.	Teacher to explain the meaning of the word '**conversion**'. Discuss together what conversion means and why the '**Book**' (**Bible**) and the '**Burden**' (**Sin**) both play a vital role in conversion.	Teacher to explain the meaning of the word '**conversion**'. Discuss together what conversion means and why the '**Book**' (**Bible**) and the '**Burden**' (**Sin**) both play a vital role in conversion.
Suggested Enrichment Activities (home/school)	Children can either add to their drawing and description of the '**Book**' or the '**Burden**'; or choose to draw and describe the one they did not do in class.	Children to write a short paragraph, with illustrations if they wish, on what the word '**heaven**' means to them.	Children to write a short paragraph, with illustrations if they wish, on what the word '**heaven**' means to them.

	KS1 (Y1/2)	**LKS2** (Y3/4)	**UKS2** (Y5/6)
Learning Objective	To understand what **conversion** is and why the **cross** is so important to the Christian faith; and what an **'Evangelist'** is.	To understand what **conversion** is and why the **cross** is so important to the Christian faith; and what an **'Evangelist'** is.	To understand what **conversion** is and why the **cross** is so important to the Christian faith; and what an **'Evangelist'** is.
Content	Chapter 2 of *The Family Pilgrim's Progress*. Focus on the characters of **'Worldly Wiseman'**, **'Legality'** and the **'Village of Morality'**. What do they represent? What does the **cross** do that **'Legality'** can't? Who is **'Evangelist'**? Why is he/she important to the **Christian**?	Chapter 2 of *The Family Pilgrim's Progress*. Focus on the characters of **'Worldly Wiseman'**, **'Legality'** and the **'Village of Morality'**. What do they represent? What does the **cross** do that **'Legality'** can't? Who is **'Evangelist'**? Why is he/she important to the **Christian**?	Chapter 2 of *The Family Pilgrim's Progress*. Focus on the characters of **'Worldly Wiseman'**, **'Legality'** and the **'Village of Morality'**. What do they represent? What does the **cross** do that **'Legality'** can't? Who is **'Evangelist'**? Why is he/she important to the **Christian**?
Key Words	Worldly Wiseman Wicket-gate Morality Cross Legality Grace Evangelist Conversion Goodwill/ Jesus Christ	Worldly Wiseman The Devil Morality Wicket-gate Legality Cross Evangelist Grace Goodwill Conversion Christian	Worldly Wiseman The Devil Morality Wicket-gate Legality Cross Evangelist Grace Goodwill Conversion Christian

Key Christian Concepts	Old Testament Law Grace
	The Cross Jesus Christ
	  Conversion
		Old Testament Law Jesus Christ
		The Cross Christian
		Grace Conversion
		  The Devil
			Old Testament Law Old and New Covenant
			The Cross Christian
			Grace Conversion
			Jesus Christ The Devil

Suggested Activities	Read Chapter 2. Display allegorical names from the story on the board. Discuss the symbolism of **'Worldly Wiseman'**, **'Legality'** and the **'Village of Morality'**. Answer the question – is it possible to be perfect? Then explain what **conversion** is and what the **cross** does that we cannot. Look at the image showing **Evangelist** pointing the way to **Christian**. Discuss what he is doing and who he represents. Children draw a picture of Evangelist and write a sentence below explaining what he does.	Read Chapter 2. Display allegorical names from the story on the board. Discuss the symbolism of **'Worldly Wiseman'**, **'Legality'** and the **'Village of Morality'**. Answer the question – is it possible to be perfect? Explain what **conversion** is and what the **cross** does that humanity can't. Look at the image showing **Evangelist** pointing the way to **Christian**. Discuss what he is doing and who he represents. Children sketch their own picture of an 'evangelist' and write 3 things that he/she does.	Read Chapter 2. Display allegorical names from the story on the board. Discuss the symbolism of **'Worldly Wiseman'**, **'Legality'** and the **'Village of Morality'**. Answer the question – is it possible to be perfect? Explain what **conversion** is and what the **cross** does that we cannot. Children write an explanation of this in their exercise books. Look at the image showing **Evangelist** pointing the way to **Christian**. Discuss what he is doing and who he represents. Children sketch their own picture of an 'evangelist' and write 5 things that he/she does and why.
Plenary	As a class, think of the different names for evangelists today. For example: **Vicar** **Minister** **Pastor** **Preacher** **Priest** **Reverend** Consider names of leaders of other religions.	As a class, think of the different names for evangelists today. For example: **Vicar** **Minister** **Pastor** **Preacher** **Priest** **Reverend** Consider names of leaders of other religions.	As a class, think of the different names for evangelists today. For example: **Vicar** **Minister** **Pastor** **Preacher** **Priest** **Reverend** Consider names of leaders of other religions. Consider how the role differs across Christian denominations/other religions.
Suggested Enrichment Activities (home/school)	Find out the names of some of the local 'evangelists'. Visit a church and meet its **'Evangelist'**. See what they can find out about what he/she does.	Find out the names of some of the local 'evangelists'. Visit a church and meet its **'Evangelist'**. See what they can find out about what he/she does.	Find out the names of some of the local 'evangelists'. Visit a church and meet its **'Evangelist'**. See what they can find out about what he/she does.

Week/Lesson 4

	KS1 (Y1/2)	LKS2 (Y3/4)	UKS2 (Y5/6)
Learning Objective	To understand the significance of the **cross** to the Christian faith and that the Christian life will have times of difficulty and suffering; and God as **Trinity** and the role of the **Holy Spirit**.	To understand the significance of the **cross** to the Christian faith and that the Christian life will have times of difficulty and suffering; and God as **Trinity** and the role of the **Holy Spirit**.	To understand the significance of the **cross** to the Christian faith and that the Christian life will have times of difficulty and suffering; and God as **Trinity** and the role of the **Holy Spirit**.
Content	Chapter 3 of *The Family Pilgrim's Progress*. Explain that **God** is **Trinity** and that the **Holy Spirit** lives in the believer to give spiritual help, strength and guidance. Focus on the scene at the **cross**. Why will **Christian** never see the 'Burden' again and what do the 'Key' and the 'Scroll' represent? Consider the **Hill Difficulty**, the **Spring of Water** and the **Bench**. What does each represent?	Chapter 3 of *The Family Pilgrim's Progress*. Explain that **God** is **Trinity** and that the **Holy Spirit** lives in the believer to give spiritual help, strength and guidance. Focus on the scene at the **cross**. Why will **Christian** never see the 'Burden' again and what do the 'Key' and the 'Scroll' represent? Consider the **Hill Difficulty** and what this represents. What do the **Spring of Water** and the **Bench** represent?	Chapter 3 of *The Family Pilgrim's Progress*. Explain that **God** is **Trinity** and that the **Holy Spirit** lives in the believer to give spiritual help, strength and guidance. Focus on the scene at the **cross**. Why will **Christian** never see the 'Burden' again and what do the 'Key' and the 'Scroll' represent? Consider the **Hill Difficulty** and what this represents. What do the **Spring of Water** and the **Bench** represent?
Key Words	Interpreter Spring of Water Burden Bench Key of Promise Cross Scroll Salvation Hill Difficulty Angels	Interpreter Spring of Water Burden Bench Key of Promise Cross Scroll Salvation Hill Difficulty Angels	Interpreter Spring of Water Burden Bench Key of Promise Cross Scroll Salvation Hill Difficulty Angels
Key Christian Concepts	God Assurance Trinity Eternal Life Holy Spirit Angels The Cross	God Assurance Trinity Eternal Life Holy Spirit Angels The Cross	God Assurance Trinity Eternal Life Holy Spirit Angels The Cross
Suggested Activities	Read Chapter 3. Children draw a picture of themselves. Above them they write **God the Father**, beside them they write **God the Son (Jesus)** and inside them they write **God the Holy Spirit**. Explain that God is **TRINITY** and that this is one way to understand how God works as three-in-one. Divide class into 4 groups. Give each group a verse to look up in the Bible (**John 3:16, 14:16, 4:14** and **Acts 14:22**). Each group to explain to class what they think their verse means.	Read Chapter 3. Children draw a picture of themselves. Above them they write **God the Father**, beside them they write **God the Son (Jesus)** and inside them they write **God the Holy Spirit**. Explain that God is **TRINITY** and that this is one way to understand how God works as three-in-one. Divide the class into 2. To one half give the 2 verses relating to the **cross/Salvation** and to the other the 2 verses relating to the **Hill Difficulty/Spring**. Children to look the verses up and copy them out. Underneath each verse they should explain what they think the verse means.	Read Chapter 3. Children draw a picture of themselves. Above them they write **God the Father**, beside them they write **God the Son (Jesus)** and inside them they write **God the Holy Spirit**. Explain that God is **TRINITY** and that this is one way to understand how God works as three-in-one. Children to look up the 4 verses for the **cross/Salvation** and the **Hill Difficulty/Spring**. Children to copy them out. What do they think these verses mean to Christians and what do the verses teach them? Consider how/why Christians will have their own 'cross' to bear in this life.
Plenary	What are **angels**? Ask class for ideas. Can they think of any examples from the Bible where angels appear?	What are **angels**? Ask class for ideas. Can they think of any examples from the Bible where angels appear?	What are **angels**? Ask class for ideas. Can they think of any examples from the Bible where angels appear?
Suggested Enrichment Activities (home/school)	Children to find out what book/s of the Bible tell us about the angel Gabriel appearing to Mary.	Children to find an example of an **angel/s** appearing in the Bible.	Children to find 3 examples of an **angel/s** appearing in the Bible.

Week/Lesson 5

	KS1 (Y1/2)	**LKS2** (Y3/4)	**UKS2** (Y5/6)
Learning Objective	To understand how the **church** supports the Christian on his/her spiritual journey; and to consider Christian belief in **good**/**evil** and **the devil**.	To understand how the **church** supports the Christian on his/her spiritual journey; and to consider Christian belief in **good**/**evil** and **the devil**.	To understand how the **church** supports the Christian on his/her spiritual journey; and to consider Christian belief in **good**/**evil** and **the devil**.
Content	Chapter 4 of *The Family Pilgrim's Progress*. Focus on **Palace Beautiful** as a symbol of the non-conformist **church**. What does it tell us about the role of the church? Consider **Christian's** fight with **Apollyon**. Who and what does **Apollyon** represent? Focus on the armour that **Christian** was given at **Palace Beautiful** and is mentioned in **Ephesians 6:14-18**. What does it symbolise and how does it help Christian?	Chapter 4 of *The Family Pilgrim's Progress*. Focus on **Palace Beautiful** as a symbol of the non-conformist **church**. What does it tell us about the role of the church then? How does it compare with today? Consider **Christian's** fight with **Apollyon**. Who and what does **Apollyon** represent? Focus on the armour that **Christian** was given at **Palace Beautiful** and is mentioned in **Ephesians 6:14-18**. What does it symbolise and how does it help Christian?	Chapter 4 of *The Family Pilgrim's Progress*. Focus on **Palace Beautiful** as a symbol of the non-conformist **church**. What does it tell us about the role of the church then? How does it compare with today? Consider **Christian's** fight with **Apollyon**. Who and what does **Apollyon** represent? Focus on the armour that **Christian** was given at **Palace Beautiful** and is mentioned in **Ephesians 6:14-18**. What does it symbolise and how does it help Christian?
Key Words	Watchful, Charity, Apollyon, Palace Beautiful / Church, Good, Evil, Spiritual Armour	Watchful, Charity, Apollyon, Palace Beautiful / Church, Good, Evil, Spiritual Armour	Watchful, Charity, Apollyon, Palace Beautiful / Church, Good, Evil, Spiritual Armour
Key Christian Concepts	Church, Charity (love) / Spiritual Armour, Apollyon/The Devil	Church, Charity (love) / Spiritual Armour, Apollyon/The Devil	Church, Charity (love), Spiritual Armour / Apollyon/The Devil, Spiritual Warfare
Suggested Activities	Read Chapter 4. Compare the **Palace Beautiful** to a stay at a 5-star hotel. What would children expect from it and how should it make them feel? Consider key words used eg. peace, love, good company, comfort, refreshment, fun, relaxation, energising… Discuss the fight between **Christian** and **Apollyon**. What does each character represent? List different words for each (good/bad, good/evil, right/wrong, **Jesus**/**devil**…) Draw and label the pieces of armour named in the verses in **Ephesians**.	Read Chapter 4. Compare the **Palace Beautiful** to a stay at a 5-star hotel. What would children expect from it and how should it make them feel? Consider key words used eg. peace, love, good company, comfort, refreshment, fun, relaxation, energising… Discuss the fight between **Christian** and **Apollyon**. What does each character represent? List different words for each (good/bad, good/evil, right/wrong, **Jesus**/**devil**…) Draw, label and describe the pieces of armour named in the verses in **Ephesians**.	Read Chapter 4. Compare the **Palace Beautiful** to a stay at a 5-star hotel. What would children expect from it and how should it make them feel? Consider key words used eg. peace, love, good company, comfort, refreshment, fun,… Discuss the fight between **Christian** and **Apollyon**. What does each character represent? List different words for each (good/bad, good/evil, right/wrong, **Jesus**/**devil**…) Draw, label and describe the pieces of armour named in the verses in **Ephesians**. How does each help Christians live the Christian life?
Plenary	Consider what the different pieces of **spiritual armour** represent. Discuss what these mean to Christians and how they help them live the Christian life.	Consider what the different pieces of **spiritual armour** represent. Discuss what these mean to Christians and how they help them live the Christian life.	Consider what the different pieces of **spiritual armour** represent. Discuss what these mean to Christians and how they help them live the Christian life.
Suggested Enrichment Activities (home/school)	Find the **Lord's Prayer** in the Bible (**Luke 11:2-4**). Copy it out (in exercise books or for display). Think about what **prayer** is and what it means to Christians. Do other religions pray?	Find the **Lord's Prayer** in the Bible (**Luke 11:2-4**). Copy it out (in exercise books or for display). Think about what **prayer** is and what it means to Christians. What do they know about other religions and **prayer**?	Find the **Lord's Prayer** in the Bible (**Luke 11:2-4**). Copy it out (in exercise books or for display). Think about what **prayer** is and what it means to Christians. What do they know about other religions and **prayer**? What are the similarities? What are the differences?

	KS1 (Y1/2)	**LKS2** (Y3/4)	**UKS2** (Y5/6)
Learning Objective	To appreciate the role of the **heart** in Christian **faith** and pilgrimage; to understand that the Christian life means putting God first and that faithfulness to God may mean suffering and sacrifice – the focus for the Christian is not on the earthly life but on the heavenly one.	To appreciate the role of the **heart** in Christian **faith** and pilgrimage; to understand that the Christian life means putting God first and that faithfulness to God may mean suffering and sacrifice – the focus for the Christian is not on the **temporal** (earthly) life but on the **eternal** (heavenly) one.	To appreciate the role of the **heart** in Christian **faith** and pilgrimage; to understand that the Christian life means putting God first and that faithfulness to God may mean suffering and sacrifice – the focus for the Christian is not on the **temporal** (earthly) life but on the **eternal** (heavenly) one.
Content	Chapter 6 of *The Family Pilgrim's Progress*. Consider the character **Talkative** and what he represents. What does this teach us about the meaning of being a **Christian**? Focus on **Vanity Fair** and the symbolism Bunyan uses. What does the Fair and its contents represent? What do the pilgrims represent? What is the message that Bunyan wants to get across here?	Chapter 6 of *The Family Pilgrim's Progress*. Consider the character **Talkative** and what he represents. What does this teach us about the meaning of being a **Christian**? Focus on **Vanity Fair** and the symbolism Bunyan uses. What does the Fair and its contents represent? What do the pilgrims represent? What is the message that Bunyan wants to get across here?	Chapter 6 of *The Family Pilgrim's Progress*. Consider the character **Talkative** and what he represents. What does this teach us about the meaning of being a **Christian**? Focus on **Vanity Fair** and the symbolism Bunyan uses. What does the Fair and its contents represent? What do the pilgrims represent? What is the message that Bunyan wants to get across here?
Key Words	Faithful / Talkative / Christian / Lord Hate-good / Vanity Fair / Heart / Faith / Suffering / Sacrifice / Heaven / Earth	Faithful / Talkative / Christian / Lord Hate-good / Vanity Fair / Heart / Faith / Suffering / Sacrifice / Heaven / Earth	Faithful / Talkative / Christian / Lord Hate-good / Vanity Fair / Martyr / Heart / Faith / Suffering / Sacrifice / Heaven / Earth
Key Christian Concepts	Heart / Faith / Sacrifice / Heaven / Earth / Christian	Heart / Faith / Sacrifice / Heaven/eternal / Earth/temporal / Christian	Heart / Faith / Sacrifice / Heaven/eternal / Earth/temporal / Christian
Suggested Activities	Briefly explain what happens in Chapter/'Story Section' 5. Read Chapter 6. Discuss **Talkative**. What is missing from his **faith**? Why is the heart vital to being a **Christian**? How do we know? In pairs, children to look at Bible verse/s which teach about the role of the **heart**. What does their verse/s tell them? Feedback. Show the class the picture of the Fair and explain where Bunyan got his inspiration from. Make a list of things that might be found at **Vanity Fair**. Why are the pilgrims prepared to die?	Briefly explain what happens in Chapter/'Story Section' 5. Read Chapter 6. Discuss **Talkative**. What is missing from his **faith**? Why is the heart vital to being a **Christian**? How do we know? In pairs, children to look at Bible verse/s which teach about the role of the **heart**. What does their verse/s tell them? Feedback. Show the class the picture of the Fair and explain where Bunyan got his inspiration from. Make a list of things that might be found at **Vanity Fair**. Why are the pilgrims prepared to die?	Briefly explain what happens in Chapter/'Story Section' 5. Then read Chapter 6. Discuss **Talkative**. What is missing from his **faith**? Why is the heart vital to being a **Christian**? How do we know? In pairs, children to look at Bible verses which teach about the role of the **heart**. What do their verses tell them? Feedback. Show the class the picture of the Fair and explain where Bunyan got his inspiration from. Make a list of things that might be found at **Vanity Fair** and another list of what matters to the pilgrims. Why are they prepared to die? What does this tell us about their faith and what it means to them?
Plenary	Discuss why **Faithful** was prepared to die. What does this tell us about the **Christian faith** and what **God** means to Christians? Relate to Bunyan's own life experience.	Discuss why **Faithful** was prepared to die. What does this tell us about the **Christian faith** and what **God** means to Christians? Relate to Bunyan's own life experience.	Discuss why **Faithful** was prepared to die. What does this tell us about the **Christian faith** and what **God** means to Christians? Are there real-life examples of people who have died for their **faith**? (Explain that Bunyan would have been inspired by one of two books he had with him in prison – Foxe's *Book of Martyrs*).
Suggested Enrichment Activities (home/school)	Find **1 Corinthians 13:13** in the Bible and copy it out. Think about what the words **Faith**, **Hope** and **Love** mean. Write down ideas.	Find **1 Corinthians 13:13** in the Bible and copy it out. Think about what the words **Faith**, **Hope** and **Love** mean. Write down ideas. What do they mean to Christians?	Find **1 Corinthians 13:13** in the Bible and copy it out. Think about what the words **Faith**, **Hope** and **Love** mean. Write down ideas. What do they mean to Christians? Do they have different meanings to different people/religions?

	KS1 (Y1/2)	LKS2 (Y3/4)	UKS2 (Y5/6)
Learning Objective	To understand that there may be times of **doubt** and despair in the Christian life, but that keeping close to God can help avoid or overcome these feelings; the importance of the **Bible**.	To understand that there may be times of **doubt** and despair in the Christian life, but that keeping close to God can help avoid or overcome these feelings; the importance of the **Bible**.	To understand that there may be times of **doubt** and despair in the Christian life, but that keeping close to God can help avoid or overcome these feelings; the importance of the **Bible**.
Content	Read Chapter 8 of *The Family Pilgrim's Progress*. Focus on the key symbolism in this chapter – **Doubting Castle**, **Giant Despair** and **Diffidence**. Consider what they represent and why Bunyan portrays them so dark and giant-like. Then consider how the pilgrims managed to escape; the importance of the **Bible** as the **Word of God**.	Read Chapter 8 of *The Family Pilgrim's Progress*. Focus on the key symbolism in this chapter – **Doubting Castle**, **Giant Despair** and **Diffidence**. Consider what they represent and why Bunyan portrays them so dark and giant-like. Then consider how the pilgrims managed to escape; the importance of the **Bible** as the **Word of God**.	Read Chapter 8 of *The Family Pilgrim's Progress*. Focus on the key symbolism in this chapter – **Doubting Castle**, **Giant Despair** and **Diffidence**. Consider what they represent and why Bunyan portrays them so dark and giant-like. Then consider how the pilgrims managed to escape; the importance of the **Bible** as the **Word of God**.
Key Words	**Giant Despair** **Doubting Castle** **Diffidence** **Bible**	**Giant Despair** **Doubting Castle** **Diffidence** **Bible**	**Giant Despair** **Doubting Castle** **Diffidence** **Bible**
Key Christian Concepts	**Faith** **Bible/ Word of God** **Doubt**	**Faith** **Bible/ Word of God** **Doubt**	**Faith** **Bible/ Word of God** **Doubt**
Suggested Activities	Briefly summarise Chapter/'Story Section' 7. Read Chapter 8. Discuss the meaning of the word '**doubt**' and different contexts in which it is used. What does it mean in relation to **faith**? Look at some visual representations of **Doubting Castle** and **Giant Despair**. Think of words to describe them. Look up, read together then copy out the verses relating to the **Key of Promise**. What do they tell us about **God**, **faith** and the importance of the **Bible**?	Briefly summarise Chapter/'Story Section' 7. Read Chapter 8. Discuss the meaning of the word '**doubt**' and different contexts in which it is used. What does it mean in relation to **faith**? Look at some visual representations of **Doubting Castle** and **Giant Despair**. Think of words to describe them. What do we learn about Bunyan's understanding of doubt? Look up, read together then copy out the verses relating to the **Key of Promise**. What do they tell us about **God**, **faith** and the importance of the **Bible**?	Briefly summarise Chapter/'Story Section' 7. Read Chapter 8. Discuss the meaning of the word '**doubt**' and different contexts in which it is used. What does it mean in relation to **faith**? Look at some visual representations of **Doubting Castle** and **Giant Despair**. Think of words to describe them. What do we learn about Bunyan's understanding of doubt? Look up, read together then copy out the verses relating to the **Key of Promise**. What do they tell us about **God**, **faith** and the importance of the **Bible**? What about when things don't turn out well?
Plenary	Consider when and how Christians use the **Bible**. (Sunday services, Bible studies, personal devotions, Christmas/Easter, births, marriages, deaths). Why is it so important to read the **Bible**?	When and how do Christians use the **Bible**? (Sunday services, Bible studies, personal devotions, Christmas/Easter, births, marriages, deaths). Why is it so important to read the **Bible**?	When and how do Christians use the **Bible**? (Sunday services, Bible studies, personal devotions, Christmas/Easter, births, marriages, deaths). Why is it so important to read the **Bible**? How might **faith** be affected if the **Bible** is not read?
Suggested Enrichment Activities (home/school)	Find **Psalm 23** in the Bible. This is one of the most well-known and used passages in the **Bible**. Copy it out and illustrate.	Find **Psalm 23** in the Bible. This is one of the most well-known and used passages in the **Bible**. Copy it out and illustrate. Children to highlight any parts of it that remind them of *The Pilgrim's Progress*.	Find **Psalm 23** in the Bible. This is one of the most well-known and used passages in the **Bible**. Copy it out and illustrate. Children to highlight any parts of it that remind them of *The Pilgrim's Progress*. Write down why they think this Psalm is often chosen for special services/ occasions.

Week/Lesson 8

	KS1 (Y1/2)	**LKS2** (Y3/4)	**UKS2** (Y5/6)
Learning Objective	To explore the meaning of 'heaven' in Christian faith and practice; to understand the importance in Christian belief of **Jesus Christ as Saviour**.	To explore the meaning of 'heaven' in Christian faith and practice; to understand the importance in Christian belief of **Jesus Christ as Saviour**.	To explore the meaning of 'heaven' in Christian faith and practice; to understand the importance in Christian belief of **Jesus Christ as Saviour**.
Content	Read Chapter 11 of *'The Family Pilgrim's Progress'*. Briefly consider the **River of Death**: what it symbolises, why it feels more difficult for some than others and what comforts are available for Christians. Focus on the **Celestial City**. What happens when the pilgrims arrive? What is the City like? And why is the **Scroll** important? Consider what makes a true pilgrim and the importance in Christian belief of **Jesus Christ as Saviour**.	Read Chapter 11 of *'The Family Pilgrim's Progress'*. Briefly consider the **River of Death**: what it symbolises, why it feels more difficult for some than others and what comforts are available for Christians. Focus on the **Celestial City**. What happens when the pilgrims arrive? What is the City like? And why is the **Scroll** important? Consider what makes a true pilgrim and the importance in Christian belief of **Jesus Christ as Saviour**.	Read Chapter 11 of *'The Family Pilgrim's Progress'*. Briefly consider the **River of Death**: what it symbolises, why it feels more difficult for some than others and what comforts are available for Christians. Focus on the **Celestial City**. What happens when the pilgrims arrive? What is the City like? And why is the **Scroll** important? Consider what makes a true pilgrim and the importance in Christian belief of **Jesus Christ as Saviour**.
Key Words	**Christian** **Hopeful** **Angels** **Beulah** **River of Death** **Celestial City/ heaven** **The Prince/ King/Jesus Christ**	**Christian** **Hopeful** **Angels** **Beulah** **River of Death** **Celestial City/ heaven** **The Prince/ King/Jesus Christ**	**Christian** **Hopeful** **Gardener** **Angels** **Enoch** **Moses** **Elijah** **Beulah** **River of Death** **Celestial City/ heaven** **The Prince/King/ Jesus Christ**
Key Christian Concepts	**Death** **Angels** **Heaven/Hell** **Salvation** **Jesus Christ as Saviour**	**Death** **Angels** **Heaven/Hell** **Salvation** **Jesus Christ as Saviour**	**Death** **Angels** **Heaven/Hell** **Salvation** **Jesus Christ as Saviour**
Suggested Activities	Briefly summarise Chap. 9 and 10 ('Story Section' 9). Read Chapter 11. Visualise the **River of Death** as both shallow and deep. Who will find it deep and why? How can it become shallower? List all the comforts God gives the Christian at the time of death. Read **Revelation 21:1-5/22-27**. What does **heaven** sound like? The Bible teaches there is only one way to heaven (see **John 3:16** and **14:6**). What is it? Copy verses. Consider the meaning of **Jesus Christ as 'Saviour'**.	Briefly summarise Chap. 9 and 10 ('Story Section' 9). Read Chapter 11. Visualise the **River of Death** as both shallow and deep. Who will find it deep and why? How can it become shallower? List all the comforts God gives the Christian at the time of death. Read **Revelation 21:1-5/22-27**. What does **heaven** sound like? In pairs, think of words to describe heaven. The Bible teaches there is only one way to heaven (see **John 3:16** and **14:6**). What is it? Copy verses and explain why Christians believe in **Jesus Christ as 'Saviour'**.	Briefly summarise Chap. 9 and 10 ('Story Section' 9). Read Chapter 11. Visualise the **River of Death** as both shallow and deep. Who will find it deep and why? How can it become shallower? List all the comforts God gives the Christian at the time of death. Read **Revelation 21:1-5/22-27**. What does **heaven** sound like? In pairs, think of words to describe heaven. The Bible teaches there is only one way to heaven (see **John 3:16** and **14:6**). What is it? Copy verses and explain why Christians believe in **Jesus Christ as 'Saviour'**. How does this impact their view of life here?
Plenary	Read **Psalm 23** (some will have copied this out as enrichment activity). Explain that this is a Psalm that is quite commonly read at funeral/memorial/Thanksgiving services. Discuss why this might be, relating to what class know about Christian belief from *The Pilgrim's Progress* and the Bible.	Read **Psalm 23** (some will have copied this out as enrichment activity). Explain that this is a Psalm that is quite commonly read at funeral/memorial/ Thanksgiving services. Discuss why this might be, relating to what class know about Christian belief from *The Pilgrim's Progress* and the Bible.	Read **Psalm 23** (some will have copied this out as enrichment activity). Explain that this is a Psalm that is quite commonly read at funeral/memorial/ Thanksgiving services. Discuss why this might be, relating to what class know about Christian belief from *The Pilgrim's Progress* and the Bible. What concepts of the Christian faith does it speak of?
Suggested Enrichment Activities (home/school)	Children to draw a picture and write a few lines describing his/her favourite part of the story.	Children to draw a picture and write a paragraph describing his/her favourite part of the story.	Children to draw a picture and write a detailed description of his/her favourite part of the story, including their understanding of the symbolism and concepts it covers.

	KS1 (Y1/2)	**LKS2** (Y3/4)	**UKS2** (Y5/6)
Learning Objective	To appreciate more about the life of John Bunyan, *The Pilgrim's Progress* and the Christian faith through a visit to Bunyan Meeting and the John Bunyan Museum.	To appreciate more about the life of John Bunyan, *The Pilgrim's Progress* and the Christian faith through a visit to Bunyan Meeting and the John Bunyan Museum.	To appreciate more about the life of John Bunyan, *The Pilgrim's Progress* and the Christian faith through a visit to Bunyan Meeting and the John Bunyan Museum.
Content	Class group/s to visit the John Bunyan Museum and Bunyan Meeting (church). A guided tour of the museum learning more about the history of the life and times of John Bunyan and experiencing what life would have been like in the 17th century. Comparing life then and now. A guided tour of Bunyan Meeting, focussing particularly on the stained glass windows and the story they tell; also key features of the church.	Class group/s to visit the John Bunyan Museum and Bunyan Meeting (church). A guided tour of the museum learning more about the history of the life and times of John Bunyan and experiencing what life would have been like in the 17th century. Comparing life then and now. A guided tour of Bunyan Meeting, focussing particularly on the stained glass windows and the story they tell; also key features of the church.	Class group/s to visit the John Bunyan Museum and Bunyan Meeting (church). A guided tour of the museum learning more about the history of the life and times of John Bunyan and experiencing what life would have been like in the 17th century. Comparing life then and now. A guided tour of Bunyan Meeting, focussing particularly on the stained glass windows and the story they tell; also key features of the church.
Key Words	Similarity/difference Century Artefact Primary source Secondary source Anvil Prison Puritan Roundhead Royalist Cavalier Pulpit **Communion** **Minister/Evangelist** **Baptism/baptistery** **Bible/Word of God**	Similarity/difference Century Artefact Primary source Secondary source Anvil Prison Puritan Roundhead Royalist Cavalier Non-conformist Editions Pulpit **Communion** **Minister/Evangelist** **Baptism/baptistery** **Bible/Word of God**	Similarity/difference Century Artefact Primary source Secondary source Anvil Prison Puritan Roundhead Royalist Cavalier Non-conformist Editions Pulpit **Communion** **Minister/Evangelist** **Baptism/baptistery** **Bible/Word of God**
Key Christian Concepts	**Communion** **Baptism** **Bible/Word of God** **Minister/Evangelist** **Christian concepts relating to the story**	**Communion** **Baptism** **Bible/Word of God** **Minister/Evangelist** **Christian concepts relating to the story**	**Communion** **Baptism** **Bible/Word of God** **Minister/Evangelist** **Christian concepts relating to the story**
Suggested Activities	A variety of options are available for school visits to the John Bunyan Museum and Bunyan Meeting, including: **Guided tours of both the Museum and the church in groups.** **Historical objects handling session** **Replica costume session** **Drama activities** **Tailored programmes as agreed with the Curator.** (See Bunyan Meeting and Museum Information page for further details)	A variety of options are available for school visits to the John Bunyan Museum and Bunyan Meeting, including: **Guided tours of both the Museum and the church in groups.** **Historical objects handling session** **Replica costume session** **Drama activities** **Tailored programmes as agreed with the Curator.** (See Bunyan Meeting and Museum Information page for further details)	A variety of options are available for school visits to the John Bunyan Museum and Bunyan Meeting, including: **Guided tours of both the Museum and the church in groups.** **Historical objects handling session** **Replica costume session** **Drama activities** **Tailored programmes as agreed with the Curator.** (See Bunyan Meeting and Museum Information page for further details)
Plenary	Discuss what the children have learnt to enrich and extend their knowledge of John Bunyan, *The Pilgrim's Progress* and the Christian faith through their visit to the John Bunyan Museum and Bunyan Meeting.	Discuss what the children have learnt to enrich and extend their knowledge of John Bunyan, *The Pilgrim's Progress* and the Christian faith through their visit to the John Bunyan Museum and Bunyan Meeting.	Discuss what the children have learnt to enrich and extend their knowledge of John Bunyan, *The Pilgrim's Progress* and the Christian faith through their visit to the John Bunyan Museum and Bunyan Meeting.
Suggested Enrichment Activities (home/school)	A piece of writing and/or a drawing about the visit to the John Bunyan Museum and Bunyan Meeting.	A piece of illustrated writing about the visit to the John Bunyan Museum and Bunyan Meeting.	A piece of illustrated writing about the visit to the John Bunyan Museum and Bunyan Meeting.

> " I will remember *The Pilgrim's Progress* because the good names in the story. I hope I will use all my life.

Week/Lesson 10

	KS1 (Y1/2)	LKS2 (Y3/4)	UKS2 (Y5/6)
Learning Objective	To consolidate key concepts/beliefs of the Christian faith learnt through a study of *The Pilgrim's Progress*.	To consolidate key concepts/beliefs of the Christian faith learnt through a study of *The Pilgrim's Progress*.	To consolidate key concepts/beliefs of the Christian faith learnt through a study of *The Pilgrim's Progress*.
Content	Revisiting key concepts learnt and the symbolism Bunyan uses for them: **Sin**/**Burden** **Jesus Christ**/**Light** Significance of the **cross** **Devil**/**Apollyon** **Heaven**/**Celestial City** Life as a **pilgrimage**	Revisiting key concepts learnt and the symbolism Bunyan uses for them: **Sin**/**Burden** **Jesus Christ**/**Light** Significance of the **cross** **Devil**/**Apollyon** **Heaven**/**Celestial City** Life as a **pilgrimage**	Revisiting key concepts learnt and the symbolism Bunyan uses for them: **Sin**/**Burden** **Jesus Christ**/**Light** Significance of the **cross** **Devil**/**Apollyon** **Heaven**/**Celestial City** Life as a **pilgrimage**
Key Words	**Apollyon** — **Cross** **Burden** — **Saviour** **Light** — **Good** **Celestial City** — **Evil** **Christian** — **Devil** **Sin** — **Heaven** **Forgiveness** — **Pilgrimage** **Jesus Christ**	**Apollyon** — **Cross** **Burden** — **Saviour** **Light** — **Grace** **Celestial City** — **Good** **Christian** — **Evil** **Sin** — **Devil** **Forgiveness** — **Heaven** **Repentance** — **Pilgrimage** **Jesus Christ**	**Apollyon** — **Cross** **Burden** — **Saviour** **Light** — **Grace** **Celestial City** — **Good** **Christian** — **Evil** **Sin** — **Devil** **Forgiveness** — **Heaven** **Repentance** — **Pilgrimage** **Jesus Christ**
Key Christian Concepts	**Christian** — **Cross** **Sin** — **Saviour** **Forgiveness** — **Devil** **Jesus Christ** — **Heaven**	**Christian** — **Cross** **Sin** — **Saviour** **Forgiveness** — **Grace** **Repentance** — **Devil** **Jesus Christ** — **Heaven**	**Christian** — **Cross** **Sin** — **Saviour** **Forgiveness** — **Grace** **Repentance** — **Devil** **Jesus Christ** — **Heaven**
Suggested Activities	Divide class into pairs/groups. Give each pair/group a concept/belief and its symbol, with some key verses from the Bible which teach us about this concept/belief. Each pair/group to create a poster/collage about their concept/symbol. Pairs/groups to present their poster/collage to the class, explaining what it shows and the belief it illustrates. Summarise key beliefs/concepts learnt through concluding whole class question/answer session.	Divide class into pairs/groups. Give each pair/group a concept/belief and its symbol, with some key verses from the Bible which teach us about this concept/belief. Each pair/group to create a poster/collage about their concept/symbol. Pairs/groups to present their poster/collage to the class, explaining what it shows and the belief it illustrates. Summarise key beliefs/concepts learnt through concluding whole class question/answer session.	Divide class into pairs/groups. Give each pair/group a concept/belief and its symbol, with some key verses from the Bible which teach us about this concept/belief. Each pair/group to create a poster/collage about their concept/symbol. Pairs/groups to present their poster/collage to the class, explaining what it shows and the belief it illustrates. Summarise key beliefs/concepts learnt through concluding whole class question/answer session.
Plenary	Discuss the meaning of the word **pilgrimage**. What has it meant for **Christian** and his companions? What does it mean to Christians generally? What does it mean for people generally?	Discuss the meaning of the word **pilgrimage**. What has it meant for **Christian** and his companions? What does it mean to Christians generally? What does it mean for people generally?	Discuss the meaning of the word **pilgrimage**. What has it meant for **Christian** and his companions? What does it mean to Christians generally? What does it mean for people generally?
Suggested Enrichment Activities (home/school)	Children to write 5 key learning points about the Christian faith that they remember most.	Children to write 5 key learning points about the Christian faith that they remember most from the story and what they think about them.	Children to write 5-10 key learning points about the Christian faith that they remember most from the story and what they think about them.

Religious Education: Suggested Scheme of Work

3.2: Outcomes

Week	**KS1** (Y1/2)	**LOWER KS2** (Y3/4)	**UPPER KS2** (Y5/6)
1	**Children will have a basic understanding of:** John Bunyan, who he was, when he lived and why he is famous His Christian beliefs and why he went to prison What inspired him to write A few facts about *The Pilgrim's Progress* What an allegory is.	**Children will have a good understanding of:** John Bunyan, who he was, when he lived and why he is famous His Christian beliefs and conversion experience and why he went to prison What inspired him to write Key facts about *The Pilgrim's Progress* What an allegory is.	**Children will have a good/sound understanding of:** John Bunyan, who he was, when he lived and why he is famous His Christian beliefs, conversion experience and how this affected him, and why he went to prison What inspired him to write Key facts about *The Pilgrim's Progress* What an allegory is and how/why Bunyan uses it in this story.
2	**Children will have a basic understanding of:** The **Bible as the Word of God** The **Bible** as a book that teaches us about what it means to be **Christian** The Christian concept of **sin** The use of allegory as an aid to understanding particularly with regard to the burden as a symbol of **sin**.	**Children will have a good understanding of:** The **Bible as the Word of God** The **Bible** as a book that teaches us about what it means to be **Christian** The Christian concept of **sin** The meaning of Christian '**conversion**' The use of allegory as an aid to understanding particularly with regard to the burden as a symbol of **sin**.	**Children will have a good/sound understanding of:** The **Bible as the Word of God** The **Bible** as a book that teaches us about what it means to be **Christian** The Christian concept of **sin** The meaning of Christian '**conversion**' The use of allegory as an aid to understanding particularly with regard to the burden as a symbol of **sin**.
3	**Children will have a basic understanding of:** The Christian meaning of 'conversion' The significance of **Christ's death on the cross** to the Christian faith What an '**Evangelist**' is.	**Children will have a good understanding of:** The Christian meaning of '**conversion**' The significance of **Christ's death on the cross** to the Christian faith and its role in Christian conversion What an '**Evangelist**' is in the Christian religion. **Children will also have considered:** The names and roles of '**Evangelists**' in other religions.	**Children will have a good/sound understanding of:** The Christian meaning of '**conversion**' The significance of **Christ's death on the cross** to the Christian faith and its role in Christian conversion What an '**Evangelist**' is in the Christian religion. **Children will also have considered:** The role of '**Evangelists**' in other religions and how the role may differ across Christian denominations/other religions.
4	**Children will have a basic understanding of:** The significance of the **Cross** to the Christian faith The expectation that the Christian life will have times of difficulty and suffering – it doesn't mean an easy life God as **Trinity** and the role of the **Holy Spirit** in the life of a Christian. **Children will also have considered:** What **angels** are and some examples of where **angels** appear in the **Bible**.	**Children will have a good understanding of:** The significance of the **Cross** to the Christian faith The expectation that the Christian life will have times of difficulty and suffering – it doesn't mean an easy life God as **Trinity** and the role of the **Holy Spirit** in the life of a Christian. **Children will also have considered:** Relevant verses from the **Bible** What **angels** are and some examples of where **angels** appear in the Bible.	**Children will have a good/sound understanding of:** The significance of the **Cross** to the Christian faith The expectation that the Christian life will have times of difficulty and suffering – it doesn't mean an easy life God as **Trinity** and the role of the **Holy Spirit** in the life of a Christian. **Children will also have considered:** Relevant verses from the **Bible** and what they teach us What angels are and some examples of where **angels** appear in the Bible.
5	**Children will have a basic understanding of:** The role of the **Church** in supporting a Christian on his/her spiritual journey Christian belief in **good and evil** and the **devil** Spiritual **'armour'** for fighting evil/the devil The passage in the **Bible** that describes this armour (**Ephesians 6:14-18**). **Children may also have considered as an enrichment activity:** **The Lord's Prayer** What **prayer** is and what it means to Christians and to other religions.	**Children will have a good understanding of:** The role of the **Church** in supporting a Christian on his/her spiritual journey Christian belief in **good and evil** and the **devil** Spiritual **'armour'** for fighting evil/the devil and what each piece represents The passage in the **Bible** that describes this armour (**Ephesians 6:14-18**). **Children may also have considered as an enrichment activity:** **The Lord's Prayer** What **prayer** is and what it means to Christians and to other religions.	**Children will have a good/sound understanding of:** The role of the **Church** in supporting a Christian on his/her spiritual journey Christian belief in **good and evil** and the **devil** Spiritual **'armour'** for fighting evil/the devil and what each piece represents The passage in the **Bible** that describes this armour (**Ephesians 6:14-18**). **Children may also have considered as an enrichment activity:** **The Lord's prayer** What **prayer** is and what it means to Christians Similarities and differences with regard to Christian belief about prayer and other religions.

Did you know?

The Pilgrim's Progress has been described as 'the Bible in another shape' (C.H. Spurgeon).

Week	KS1 (Y1/2)	LOWER KS2 (Y3/4)	UPPER KS2 (Y5/6)
6	**Children will have a basic understanding of:** The role the **heart** plays in Christian faith What the **Bible** teaches about putting God first in this life, even if it means suffering; and the examples of **Faithful** and Bunyan, both of whom suffered for their faith The meaning of the word 'martyr' The meaning of the earthly life and the heavenly life and what should matter most to Christians. **Children may also have considered as part of an enrichment activity:** The meaning of the words **Faith**, **Hope** and **Love**.	**Children will have a good understanding of:** The role the **heart** plays in Christian faith What the **Bible** teaches about putting God first in this life, even if it means suffering; and the examples of **Faithful** and Bunyan, both of whom suffered for their faith The meaning of the **temporal (earthly)** life and **eternal (heavenly)** life and what should matter most to Christians. **Children may also have considered as part of an enrichment activity:** The meaning of the words **Faith**, **Hope** and **Love** and their significance to Christians.	**Children will have a good/sound understanding of:** The role the **heart** plays in Christian faith What the **Bible** teaches about putting God first in this life, even if it means suffering; and the examples of **Faithful** and Bunyan, both of whom suffered for their faith The meaning of the word 'martyr' The meaning of the **temporal (earthly)** life and **eternal (heavenly)** life and what should matter most to Christians. **Children may also have considered as part of an enrichment activity:** The meaning of the words **Faith**, **Hope** and **Love** and their significance to Christians. The meaning of these words to other religions – similarities and differences.
7	**Children will have a basic understanding of:** The meaning of '**doubt**' in relation to God and faith How this might make a Christian feel The importance of keeping close to God in order to prevent/overcome feelings of doubt The role of the **Bible** in helping Christians keep close to God and strong in their faith. **Children may also have considered as part of an enrichment activity:** **Psalm 23** and why it is a commonly used passage from the **Bible**.	**Children will have a good understanding of:** The meaning of '**doubt**' in relation to God and faith How this might make a Christian feel The importance of keeping close to God in order to prevent/overcome feelings of doubt The role of the **Bible** in helping Christians keep close to God and strong in their faith. **Children may also have considered as part of an enrichment activity:** **Psalm 23**, why it is a commonly used passage from the **Bible** and what parts remind them of *The Pilgrim's Progress*.	**Children will have a good/sound understanding of:** The meaning of '**doubt**' in relation to God and faith How this might make a Christian feel The importance of keeping close to God in order to prevent/overcome feelings of doubt The role of the **Bible** in helping Christians keep close to God and strong in their faith. **Children may also have considered as part of an enrichment activity:** **Psalm 23**, why it is a commonly used passage from the **Bible**, what parts remind them of *The Pilgrim's Progress*, and why it is often chosen for special services.
8	**Children will have a basic understanding of:** The Christian concept of **heaven** The Christian belief in **Jesus Christ as 'Saviour'** What the **Bible** says about both from 3 key verses/passages – **John 3:16** and **14:6**, **Revelation 21**. **Children will also have considered:** **Psalm 23** and the aspects of the Christian faith that are referred to in this Psalm.	**Children will have a good understanding of:** The Christian concept of **heaven** The Christian belief in **Jesus Christ as 'Saviour'** What the **Bible** says about both from 3 key verses/passages – **John 3:16** and **14:6**, **Revelation 21**. **Children will also have considered:** **Psalm 23** and the aspects of the Christian faith that are referred to in this Psalm.	**Children will have a good/sound understanding of:** The Christian concept of **heaven** The Christian belief in **Jesus Christ as 'Saviour'** What the **Bible** says about both from 3 key verses/passages – **John 3:16** and **14:6**, **Revelation 21** How these beliefs impact the **Christian life**; and Christian attitudes to **life and death**. **Children will also have considered:** **Psalm 23** and the aspects of the Christian faith that are referred to in this Psalm.
9	**Children will have a basic understanding and appreciation of:** The difference between Primary and Secondary sources The similarities and differences between life in John Bunyan's time and 21st century How the study of Bunyan, *The Pilgrim's Progress* and the Christian faith can be enriched through visiting the museum and church.	**Children will have a good understanding of:** The difference between Primary and Secondary sources The similarities and differences between life in John Bunyan's time and 21st century How the study of Bunyan, *The Pilgrim's Progress* and the Christian faith can be enriched through visiting the museum and church.	**Children will have a good/sound understanding of:** The difference between Primary and Secondary sources The similarities and differences between life in John Bunyan's time and 21st century How the study of Bunyan, *The Pilgrim's Progress* and the Christian faith can be enriched through visiting the museum and church.
10	**Children will have consolidated their understanding of the following key Christian concepts/beliefs:** Sin · Jesus Christ as Saviour The cross · Devil/Good and Evil Heaven · Pilgrimage	**Children will have consolidated their understanding of the following key Christian concepts/beliefs:** Sin · Jesus Christ as Saviour The cross · Devil/Good and Evil Heaven · Pilgrimage	**Children will have consolidated their understanding of the following key Christian concepts and beliefs:** Sin · Jesus Christ as Saviour The cross · Devil/Good and Evil Heaven · Pilgrimage

3.2 | Outcomes

Creative Curriculum Map

HISTORY

John Bunyan's life (1628 – 1688)

History of *The Pilgrim's Progress*

Stuart Times:
- English Civil War (1642 – 1649)
- Great Plague (1665)
- Great Fire of London (1666)
- The Puritans
- The Great Ejection (1662)
- The Glorious Revolution (1688)
- Oliver Cromwell

PHSE/SMSC

Impact of faith on citizenship

Inclusion – pilgrimage as universal concept.

Allegory – names to describe good and bad characteristics

Cultural interpretations of *The Pilgrim's Progress*

Non-conformity and citizenship

Freedom of speech, freedom of religion

SEAL – impact of story on individuals/class (personal/subjective – impersonal/objective)

John Bunyan and *The Pilgrim's Progress*

ART/DESIGN

Stained glass windows

Collage

Sketching/painting (characters/scenes)

Calligraphy

Palace Beautiful (interior design)

Map of Christian's journey

RELIGIOUS EDUCATION

God as Trinity

Creation/the Fall

The Gospel message

Sin

Salvation

Eternal life and biblical teaching on Heaven and Hell

Faith and Doubt

Good and Evil/the devil

Angels

Prayer

The Christian Life

Pilgrimage

The Bible

Related Bible verses/texts/stories/themes

Impact of faith – personal, family, community, world

LEARNING OUTSIDE THE CLASSROOM

Sites associated with Bunyan's life – Bedford/around Bedfordshire

Bunyan Meeting and the John Bunyan Museum

Theatre productions of *The Pilgrim's Progress*

Stained glass windows depicting scenes from Bunyan's works (Bedford/Elstow/London)

Civil War sites/museums

Oliver Cromwell's house, Ely.

LOCAL HISTORY

(see particularly *Travel with John Bunyan* by John Pestall)

Sites associated with Bunyan – his book and his life, including:

- Elstow – Parish Church, Moot Hall, Village Green
- Bedford – Bunyan Meeting and the John Bunyan Museum, Bunyan statue, sites of County and Bedford Gaols, Bunyan's home in St. Cuthbert's Street, St John's Church and Rectory, Swan Hotel, River Ouse
- Ampthill and surrounding hills – Houghton House (Palace Beautiful) and Hill Difficulty
- Stevington – the cross and church well
- Chiltern Hills – Delectable Mountains and Immanuel's Land
- Millbrook – Valley of the Shadow of Death

GEOGRAPHY

Local Map of Bedford/Bedfordshire – find Bunyan landmarks

Compare with old map of Bedfordshire

OS Map, Bedfordshire: locate sites relating to Bunyan and *The Pilgrim's Progress*

Grid references: OS map of Bedfordshire.

Create own maps of *The Pilgrim's Progress* and Christian's journey

Bunyan as tourist attraction for Bedford/Bedfordshire – create general leaflet/marketing materials

EXTENSION/ENRICHMENT

Independent Project Work

Research/Enrichment Studies. Potential to link with Bunyan Meeting and the John Bunyan Museum, and/or local universities/relevant organisations

ICT

Film/animated versions of *The Pilgrim's Progress* – study changes/developments in technology and presentation

Use technology to create own dramatization of chapter/scene/window

LITERACY

Allegory, metaphor, simile

The Historical Novel

Biography/Autobiography

Language – 17th century text, compare original text with modern, also original with children's versions

Description/narrative

Comprehension activities – *The Pilgrim's Progress* and the Bible

Story writing – A Day in My Life (using allegorical names/symbolism)

Other works by Bunyan, especially *The Pilgrim's Progress: Part II*

Bunyan's hymn – vocabulary/versions/history

Reading the original version/language

Comparing children's editions of *The Pilgrim's Progress*

DRAMA

Bunyan's story – his arrest, character, preaching

Enacting parts of *The Pilgrim's Progress* – by chapter, scene, window

Observing/critiquing dramatic productions (film/theatre/audio)

MUSIC

John Bunyan's hymn

Music in Bunyan's day

Development of the hymn in worship

3.5: Glossary
Key Christian words and concepts

Angels	Divine beings. There are good angels and fallen angels. The Bible teaches that good angels are sent by God to watch over us. It was the angel Gabriel who visited Mary to tell her that she was to bear the baby Jesus, God's son.
Apollyon	The enemy of God, a fallen angel who desires the destruction of God's kingdom and the souls of humanity. Apollyon (also known as the devil or Satan) fights to keep believers and non-believers away from God. The devil is also called Captain Beelzebub by Bunyan.
Apostle	The name/title given to Christ's twelve disciples. It means one who is sent as messenger. After the Resurrection the original group was enlarged.
Assurance	The certainty of salvation that, once obtained, cannot be taken away.
Bible	The Word of God. The Bible is the sacred book of Christianity. It is divided into two main parts – the Old and New Testaments. There are 66 books of the Bible, each one divided into chapters and verses.
Christ	The Son of God, part of the triune God (Trinity). Also known as Jesus or Jesus Christ, Immanuel, God with us, the Word. Christ came down to earth as a baby and took on human form. His life is documented in the four Gospels (**Matthew**, **Mark**, **Luke** and **John**). He was crucified on a cross to atone for the sins of humanity, fulfilling Old Testament prophecy. At Easter Christians celebrate Christ's death and resurrection.
Christian	Someone who has repented of their sin and committed their life to following Jesus Christ and the Word of God.
Communion	A communion service is where bread and wine are served in remembrance of Christ and his death on the cross.
Conversion	The moment when a person becomes 'Christian'. This is when regeneration (a spiritual new birth) takes place. Some people can name the day/time that this took place, whilst for others (like Bunyan) knowledge of their 'assurance' of regeneration takes time. This is why Bunyan portrays conversion as both a process (Christian) and instantaneous (Hopeful). Christians will have different conversion experiences. Whilst Christian became 'Christian' at the Wicket-gate (his moment of conversion), he doesn't realise this until he gets to the cross where he loses his burden.
Creation	When the world was created. The Bible teaches that creation took place over 6 days with the seventh day being the day God rested. The creation account is found in **Genesis**, the first book of the Bible.
Cross	Jesus Christ was crucified on the cross. The cross is an important Christian symbol as it signifies the moment when humanity was offered the hope of eternal life through Christ's death and resurrection.
Death	The end of this mortal life, something everyone must experience.
Devil	See **Apollyon**.
Doubt	A lack of certainty. In Christian terms, this can mean doubting God and his presence/action in one's life, or doubting the very existence of God. This latter type of doubt Bunyan himself experienced, describing it as doubt of the worst kind in his book *Grace Abounding*.
Eternal Life	Life after death that will never end. Christianity teaches that eternal life will either be with God (heaven) or without (hell).
Evangelism	Telling others about one's faith. In Christianity this links to the word 'evangelical', the meaning of which incorporates 'activism' – proactively sharing faith with others. This word also links with the word 'Evangelist' – a formal name for someone who shares their faith with others (although the word particularly relates to ministers/preachers etc, it can be applied to anyone who does this, not just to those appropriately employed or trained).
Faith	Belief in something unseen. For Christians, this means a belief in God as Trinity (God the Father, God the Son and God the Holy Spirit) and in the Word of God.
Fall	When Adam and Eve succumbed to the temptation of Satan and went against God's command, taking fruit from the Tree of the Knowledge of Good and Evil in the Garden of Eden. This is the moment when sin and death entered the world. The account of the Fall is found in **Genesis 3**.
Fellowship	Christian companionship, friendship, support and encouragement. The Bible stresses the importance of Christian fellowship. This is why Christians are encouraged to attend/become a member of a church.
Forgiveness	Christianity teaches that to be Christian it is necessary to repent of sin (to say sorry for) and ask forgiveness from God. Forgiveness means to pardon and be pardoned. Forgiveness is a key theme throughout the Bible.
Glorification	The realisation of the promise of eternal life, the moment when the Christian enters heaven and is 'glorified' with Christ.
God	The Creator, the supreme being. The Bible teaches that God is TRINITY – three in one: God the Father, God the Son and God the Holy Spirit.
God's Promises	Found in the Bible. The Bible is full of verses that assure the Christian of God's promise – salvation by faith. The better we know and understand the Bible the more we are able to call upon these promises in times of trouble. Promises are there to guide as well as to comfort/assure.
Gospel	The glad tidings or good news of the promise of the Kingdom of God as preached by Christ. **Matthew**, **Mark**, **Luke** and **John** are the first 4 books of the New Testament and tell the story of Christ's birth, life, ministry and death – hence they are called the Gospels.
Grace	Describes Christ's sacrifice on the cross and the forgiveness of sins for all true believers.
Heart	The Bible explicitly connects the heart with faith in both the Old and New Testament. To be a Christian involves a commitment from the heart as well as the head/mind.
Heaven	The Bible teaches that Christian believers will spend an eternity with God in Heaven (see **Revelation**).

Hell	An eternity without God often symbolised in the Bible by fire.
Holy Spirit	Part of the Trinity, the triune God. The Holy Spirit lives in all believers and acts as spiritual guide, interpreter and helper. The Bible teaches that Christians receive the Holy Spirit on conversion.
Hope	The biblical 'hope' refers to the hope that Christians have through the death of Christ on the cross which offers forgiveness of sins and the promise of eternal life for all who believe.
Incarnation	When Christ took on human form, born as a baby to Mary in Bethlehem.
Jesus	The Son of God. See **Christ**.
Judgement Day	The Bible teaches that everyone will be judged at the end of time.
Justification	Justification means to be 'justified' in the sight of God through repentance and forgiveness of sin. Justification occurs at the point of conversion.
Law	This refers to the Old Testament law given to Moses, and includes the Ten Commandments. This was the Old Covenant between God and his people to help direct them to live good lives and honour God. With the coming of the New Covenant (Christ/grace) the need for the Old Covenant was abolished, though it is still a useful guide.
Light	Symbolic of the Word of God and also of Christ. Light as a symbol representing goodness/Christ/the Word is used frequently in the Bible.
Lord's Supper	See also **Communion**. The first Lord's Supper was shared by Christ with his twelve disciples just before he was arrested. The bread and wine remind Christians of Jesus, his body and his blood.
Love	The greatest of the three Christian/theological virtues (see **1 Corinthians 13:13**).
Mercy	The forgiveness and compassion shown by God in sending his Son, Jesus Christ, to become Saviour of the world. The Bible teaches that only Christ has the power to save.
Mission	Sharing the Word of God with others. The word 'missionary' stems from this word – a missionary devotes his/her life to telling others about God either directly or through a particular occupation.
New Testament	The Bible is divided into two main sections – the Old and the New Testament. The New Testament records Christ's birth, life, ministry, death and resurrection and the work/letters of his apostles that followed him. The NT contains 27 books.
Obedience	Doing as one is directed. In the Christian faith this means following/being obedient to the Word of God and actively aspiring to lead a holy life.
Old Testament	The first of the two main sections of the Bible. The Old Testament contains 39 of the 66 books of the Bible and includes prophecies of the coming of Christ.
Patience	Quiet endurance/waiting for something. The Bible encourages Christians to be patient – with God and with others.
Prayer	Talking to/communion with God. The Bible teaches that we can pray directly to God and that we should pray continually. Prayers should include praise, thanksgiving, repentance and requests.
Providence	This means God-given/provided. The Bible teaches that God is in control of everything – events happen within the 'providence' of God.
Repentance	Saying sorry. The Bible teaches that repentance should be heart-felt.
Resurrection	When Jesus rose again/came back to life. Christians celebrate the resurrection of Christ on Easter Sunday.
Salvation	The saving of the soul through deliverance from sin and its consequences by the death of Christ on the cross.
Sanctification	Means the Christian pilgrimage, or journey, of faith. As we progress in faith, keep close to Christ and desire to be like him, we are gradually being 'sanctified'.
Satan	Another word for the devil. See **Apollyon**.
Sovereignty	God's sovereignty means that God is ultimately in control of everything.
Spiritual Armour	Spiritual weapons for the protection of Christians: breastplate of righteousness, shield of faith, helmet of salvation, sword of the Spirit (see **Ephesians 6**).
Spiritual Warfare	When the devil fights to keep believers and non-believers away from God. Spiritual warfare is terrible but it works for the good of Christians, aiding them in their spiritual growth and proving their faith.
Temporal	Refers to the earthly life which is only temporary, in contrast with the heavenly life, which is eternal.
Trinity	The Triune God – three persons in one. Christianity is the only faith that has a triune God – God the Father, God the Son and God the Holy Spirit.
Wisdom	Knowledge and sound judgement/understanding in spiritual matters. Wisdom is often connected with age as it is gained through experience, but not always. Sometimes younger people/Christians can be wiser than the more mature. The Bible teaches that wisdom is to be valued and treasured.
Witness	The Bible teaches that Christians should tell others about Christ, to be 'witnesses' of Christ and the Gospel, as the apostles were.
Word of God	The Bible, God's word. The Christian's most valuable spiritual guide. See **Bible**.

FAITHFUL
HELPING CHRISTIAN

> "I have enjoyed studying *The Pilgrim's Progress* because I've learnt lots more about what a pilgrim is. I never used to know what a pilgrim is now I know its about following Jesus and going to God. I will remember lots but especially remember the song we sang at the church/museum. The song was called 'Who would valour see'.

Chapter 4
Resources Information

Well Faithful, thou has faithfully professed
Unto thy Lord: with him thou shall be blessed;
When faithless ones, with all their vain delights,
Are crying out under their hellish plights.
Sing, Faithful, sing; and let thy name survive;
For though they killed thee, thou art yet alive.

BUNYAN MEETING

Bunyan Meeting and the John Bunyan Museum
Learning outside the classroom

Mill Street
Bedford
MK40 3EU

Bunyan Meeting and the John Bunyan Museum & Library are housed in a cluster of historic buildings in the centre of Bedford and are open throughout the year for school visits.

The present church building was completed in 1850 and is particularly famous for the 8 beautiful stained-glass windows depicting scenes from the life of John Bunyan and his world-famous allegory *The Pilgrim's Progress* and the bronze doors given to the Church in 1876 by the 9th Duke of Bedford, which also depict scenes from *The Pilgrim's Progress*. The present John Bunyan Museum opened in 1998 and offers the visitor an excellent tour through the life and times of John Bunyan, including significant artefacts associated with the 17th century preacher, pastor and author.

Bunyan Meeting
A brief history

On 21st January 1672, just weeks before his release from prison, John Bunyan was appointed Pastor of the Bedford Independent church once led by the Rev. John Gifford. He was to be the fifth pastor of the church now known as Bunyan Meeting.

Since its eviction from St John's church in 1660, this small congregation had been without a place of worship in which to meet. In May 1672, a member of the congregation purchased an orchard and barn in Mill Lane, close to the church of St Cuthbert's (where Bunyan's son Joseph was christened in November 1672) and to Bunyan's own cottage on St Cuthbert's Street. The barn was then sold to the church for £50, converted for use as a place of worship and licensed for preaching. Such was the popularity of John Bunyan, on the day the new 'church' was opened the meeting had to take place in the open air as so many people gathered there to be part of the occasion.

This converted barn was to be the place of worship for the Bedford congregation for 35 years. In 1707 it was replaced by a three gabled building seating 700 people and known as the 'Old Meeting'. The current building , known as Bunyan Meeting, was built in 1850 at a cost of £3,400. A number of changes to this building have been made over time, including:

Left: The bronze doors.

Opposite (top left): Bunyan Meeting and the communion table, believed to be the original table used by John Bunyan.

Opposite (top right): A scene from the bronze doors.

Opposite (bottom): School children studying one of the stained glass windows at Bunyan Meeting.

- **The bronze doors**. These were gifted to the church by the 9th Duke of Bedford in 1876. These famous doors have ten panels depicting scenes from *The Pilgrim's Progress* and were made by the sculptor Frederick Thrupp. The doors took three years to make and were exhibited at the Royal Academy before being purchased by Francis Hastings Russell, 9th Duke of Bedford, and presented to Bunyan Meeting. The doors now provide a fitting entrance to the church once pastored by the author of *The Pilgrim's Progress*.

- **The stained glass windows**. These would not have been allowed at the time of Bunyan as he and other non-conformists believed very much in the need for simplicity in church life. The eight stained glass windows in the Sanctuary were installed at different times during the 20th and 21st centuries, with the green window depicting Faithful and Christian being the first and the Apollyon window the last to be installed. These windows are stunning visual representations of key scenes from *The Pilgrim's Progress*.

- **The pews**. The original wooden pews were removed in the later part of the twentieth century and replaced with more modern, versatile seating. This enables the Sanctuary to be used for a greater variety of services. Original wooden pews remain in the gallery which is used every Sunday morning and for special services.

- **The walls and woodwork of the Sanctuary**. These have been painted to give a fresher, more contemporary and welcoming interior.

72

Also of note to see/discuss on a visit to the church:

· **The pulpit**. This is central to the church as the non-conformists believed that God's Word, the Bible, is central to Christian belief and the Christian life.

· **The original communion table** used by John Bunyan.

· **The baptistry and the font**. Although neither are on view it is worthwhile to point out that Bunyan Meeting believes in both infant baptism and adult baptism. It therefore has a font that is brought into the church for christenings and a baptistry (under the communion table) that can be used for baptism by immersion.

· **The organ**. The original organ was housed in the gallery immediately above the pulpit. Although the organ is now at the front of the church, the pipework can still be seen in its original situation. The organ console is still used in services each week and for special services.

· **The Memorial Plaques** either side of the pulpit, commemorating members of Bunyan Meeting who died in World Wars I and II.

· **A record of the Pastors/Ministers of Bunyan Meeting** in chronological order can be seen inscribed around the frame of the stained glass window showing Evangelist (John Gifford) 'pointing the way' to Christian (John Bunyan). This record is being continued around the frame of the window depicting Christian and Hopeful arriving at the Celestial City.

> " My favourite thing at the church is asking questions to Peter.

The John Bunyan Museum

The John Bunyan Museum & Library collection was started following John Bunyan's death in 1688 and has developed over the intervening years. The collection developed from a few core items, and grew during the life of Bunyan Meeting. Today this is the most important Bunyan collection in the world, containing almost all the existing objects with personal connection to John Bunyan, and is one of the leading Bunyan libraries, containing the largest number of foreign language editions. The first museum was set up in 1946 and continued to collect items, mainly through public donations.

Following extensive work the new purpose-built John Bunyan Museum was opened in 1998 and has a number of significant artefacts on display relating to John Bunyan, his life, times and works. It also has a waxwork replica of John Bunyan and a small prison cell much like the one where Bunyan would have spent his long imprisonment. The Museum is led by a curator and offers schools a variety of opportunities and activities. It has a large number of trained volunteers who are available for guided tours of both the church and museum. There are also additional facilities for lunch and/or further learning activities, depending on school requirements.

A standard visit will include:
a 30 minute guided tour of the museum, a 30 minute guided tour of the church using the stained glass windows to tell the story of *The Pilgrim's Progress*, and a 30 minute 'historical objects' handling session. Additional time in both the museum and the church is possible for students to browse and/or complete activities, if required.

An additional/optional activity:
30 minutes replica costume session 'John and Elizabeth Bunyan'.

If you have particular requirements for your visit, for example, a focus on an identified area of the curriculum (History, Local History, Religious Education, Literacy, Art) the Curator will be happy to discuss your requirements with you.

Occasionally special events are organised at the church/museum. These will be advertised on the website: www.bunyanmeeting.co.uk/museum

Outreach sessions are also available. These include costume and historical objects handling sessions. There is a charge per session plus mileage. For details of outreach sessions, or if schools would like to organise a teacher-training session, please contact the John Bunyan Museum www.bunyanmeeting.co.uk/museum (booking forms for outreach sessions are available to download from the website).

Opening Times for Schools:
9.30am to 3.30pm
by prior arrangement

Facilities:

Church and museum shop, coffee shop, disabled access, toilets, coach drop-off point, additional rooms for hire (lunch, planned activities).

Souvenir 'goody' bags can be ordered in advance prior to your visit. Information is included in the booking pack.

Cost: There is a small charge per pupil for school visits, with an extra charge for additional room hire and/ or souvenir 'goody' bags, if required.

Bookings:

Tel: 01234 270303
Email: curator@bunyanmeeting.co.uk
www.bunyanmeeting.co.uk/museum

> " I enjoyed studying *The Pilgrim's Progress* because of all the characters and when Christian takes the wrong path. My day was great in the museum. I will remember everything because that's how good it was.

Resources for Schools

The resources listed below are all resources that can be used directly in the classroom when teaching John Bunyan and *The Pilgrim's Progress*, or as background reading/information. Many of these are on display and available for purchase at Bunyan Meeting/John Bunyan Museum.

Suggested Biographies:

The People's Pilgrim by Peter Morden (Surrey, UK: CWR, 2013)

In the Steps of John Bunyan by Vera Brittain (London: Rich and Cowan, 1950)

John Bunyan by John Brown (London: Hulbert Publishing Company, 1928)

The Pilgrim's Progress – Children's Editions:

The Family Pilgrim's Progress – Retold by Jean Watson (Scotland: Christian Focus Publications, 2007) Hardback.

The Pilgrim's Progress – Retold by Jean Watson (Scotland: Christian Focus Publications, 2009) Paperback, with Bible study activities.

Pilgrim's Progress – Retold by Tim Dowley (England: Candle Books, 2008)

Dangerous Journey – Oliver Hunkin/Yorkshire Television Ltd (USA: William B. Eerdmans Publishing Co.,1985)

A Pilgrim's Progress – Retold by Geraldine McCaughrean (London: Hodder Children's Books, 1999)

Pilgrim – Mark Jeffery (Surrey: Onwards and Upwards Publishers, 2014) A science-fiction interpretation.
(This may appeal as a follow–up/comparison reader for the class or for children who enjoy science fiction)

The Pilgrim's Progress – Complete Editions

The Pilgrim's Progress – Oxford World Classics, edited by W.R. Owens (Oxford: OUP, 2003)

Media productions/DVDs:

John Bunyan's *Dangerous Journey*, Yorkshire Television 1985 (available on YouTube)

The Pilgrim's Progress, Saltmine Theatre Company, Saltmine Trust 2011 www.saltminetrust.org.uk
(available as DVD/live theatre production – see Saltmine website)

The Pilgrim's Progress, retold by Scott Cawthon (2005)

The John Bunyan Story, Torchlighters.org

John Bunyan, The People's Pilgrim, docudrama DVD (CTA/CWR, 2016)

Additional Useful Resources:

Teacher's Resource Pack – John Bunyan Museum (includes background information and a variety of activity sheets)

Travel with John Bunyan, John Pestall (Leominster: Day One Publications, 2002)

Horrible Histories: Slimy Stuarts, Terry Deary (London: Scholastic Ltd, 1996)

Please note: A variety of additional resources/souvenirs are available for purchase from the John Bunyan Museum. These include: a map of Old Bedfordshire, postcards of the stained glass windows in Bunyan Meeting and various images from the museum, plus a variety of stationery/gift items.
Many of the books and DVD's listed above are also available for purchase from the Museum.

4.1 | Bunyan Meeting and Museum

The Pilgrim's Progress:
The Frieze

A visual representation using the windows from Bunyan Meeting, Bedford.

Information about the frieze with ideas for use within the school or classroom.

The frieze has been designed to give teachers and children a visual representation of the story using images from the stunning stained glass windows in Bunyan Meeting, Bedford. For schools close enough to Bunyan Meeting and the John Bunyan Museum, a visit is very much recommended; for those too far, this frieze at least enables you to appreciate them from afar and gives a visual flavour of the story as it is portrayed through stained glass. Incorporated within the design are:

• key words and symbolism from Bunyan's allegory

• Christian concepts

• related verses and texts from the Bible, the ultimate authority for the Christian life for Bunyan and for Christians world-wide.

The frieze is made up of 5 main sections:

Left-side:

The window showing Bunyan in his prison cell, writing 'The Pilgrim's Progress' with quill and ink.

Main section:

The story portrayed through images using the stained glass windows, symbolism from *The Pilgrim's Progress* and related Bible verses, texts and key Christian concepts.

Above:

The famous opening line of the original text. This explains that the story is written in the context of a dream, with the dreamer (Bunyan) looking on and narrating the story.

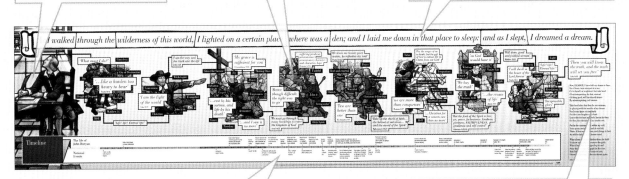

Below:

Timeline of Bunyan's life and national events.

Right-side:

The concluding poem from the original text. Here Bunyan re-iterates the importance of the message from his allegory and encourages his readers to 'preserve the gold'. He also hints of another dream/story (Part II, first published in 1684).

Some suggestions for using the frieze within the school/classroom

The frieze is designed for use within the classroom to give children a visual representation of the story using windows from Bunyan's own church (though these would not have been there in Bunyan's day). The frieze could simply be displayed as an aid to teaching the story, or there may be room around it for children's work to be displayed, dependent on how the story is being taught. Teachers will want to be creative with this, but I include just a few examples for stimulus:

Religious Education

Visuals from the story with explanations of symbolism used and Christian concepts.

Bible verses/texts relevant to each part of the story with explanations (can use those on the frieze, others included in the 'Story Sections' and/or other relevant verses – a good enrichment activity).

As the story progresses, display children's thoughts on the Christian faith and how it impacts life here on earth for 'pilgrims' (then and now).

Compare (and display) key concepts and stages on the journey with how other faiths might interpret them.

Literacy

Writing about each stage of the story, with illustrations.

Symbolism/Allegory/Adjectives.

Story work/creative writing inspired by the story as a whole or parts of it, perhaps relating to modern life or to other stories.

History/Local History/Geography

John Bunyan's life explored.

Local history sites relating to/inspiration for the story.

Sites local to your own location which could be inspiration for places within the story (for example: your own local inspiration for Palace Beautiful, Slough of Despond, Doubting Castle, Hill Difficulty, Delectable Mountains, the cross).

Art

Other stained glass windows from around the country/world portraying scenes from *The Pilgrim's Progress*.

Designing a stained glass window showing a scene from the story.

Illustrations of the story by the children.

Illustrations of scenes used in publications of *The Pilgrim's Progress* (a good research project).

'*When you pass through the waters, I will be with you, and through the rivers, they shall not overwhelm you.*' (Isaiah 43:2)

'Now when they were come up to the gate, there was written over it, in letters of gold, *Blessed are they that do his commandments, that they may have right to the Tree of Life; and may enter in through the gates into the City.*' (Revelation 22:14) (AV)

Bibliography

The Pilgrim's Progress – Children's Editions

Watson, Jean, *The Family Pilgrim's Progress* (UK: Scripture Union, 1983)

Watson, Jean, *The Family Pilgrim's Progress* (Scotland: Christian Focus Publications, 2007)

McCaughrean, Geraldine, *A Pilgrim's Progress* (London: Hodder Children's Books, 1999)

Dowley, Tim, *Pilgrim's Progress* (Oxford: Lion Hudson/Candle Books, 2008)

Hunkin, Oliver, *Dangerous Journey* (Oxford/USA: Lion Hudson/William B. Eerdmans Publishing Co, original text copyright Yorkshire Television, 1985)

Jeffery, Mark, *Pilgrim* (Surrey, UK: Onwards and Upwards Publishers, 2014)

Blyton, Enid, *The Land of Far Beyond* (Dorset, UK: Element Books, 1998)

John Bunyan – Books

Bunyan, John, *The Pilgrim's Progress*, ed. W.R. Owens (Oxford: Oxford University Press, 2003)

Bunyan, John, *Works, Volume III*, ed. George Offor (London: Blackie and Son, 1856)

Bunyan, John, *Grace Abounding* (USA: Whitaker House, 1993)

John Bunyan – Biographies

Morden, Peter, *The People's Pilgrim* (Surrey, UK: CWR, 2013)

Brittain, Vera, *In the Steps of John Bunyan* (London: Rich and Cowan, 1950, reprinted 1987)

Brown, John, *John Bunyan* (London: The Hulbert Publishing Company, 1928)

John Bunyan – Reference Books

Horner, Barry E., *Pilgrim's Progress Themes and Issues* (Darlington, England: Evangelical Press, 2003)

Pestall, John, *Travel with John Bunyan* (Leominster, UK: Day One Publications, 2002, reprinted 2005)

The Holy Bible

The Holy Bible: New International Version (Bible Gateway)

The Holy Bible: Authorised King James Version (Grand Rapids, Michigan: Zondervan Publishing House)

Education Materials

The Agreed Syllabus for Religious Education, 2012-2017 (Bedford Borough, Central Bedfordshire and Luton SACRE's and RE Today Services, 2011)